ORMSKIRK
and
THE ORIGIN OF
THE WORLD

ELAINE KENNEDY-DUBOURDIEU

Cover artwork by Elaine Kennedy-Dubourdieu
Cover design and formatting by Softwood Self Publishing

Printed by Amazon, UK

ISBN 979-8-3919-8882-3 (paperback)

For my mother and my child,
who both deserved so much better.

CONTENTS

'The past is not dead.

It is not even past'

William Faulkner

June 2016

'We love you to the moon and bag'. A white paper bag with a yellow heart and stars all over it: *Usa esta bolsa en caso de mareo y avisanos*. Use this bag if you are feeling sick and let us know.' I write on the white paper, on the front and on the back of the bag, then I open it up and try to write on the shiny bit inside. The bit that's supposed to hold the sick snug and dry. But there isn't enough room.

'Do you need that?' I ask the other passengers on this Alicante flight who are awake. And if they aren't, I lean across their laps and yank their moon bags out of the pockets in front of them. The embryos of my story. 'An emergency,' I whisper. 'I've got to write this down.'

CHAPTER ONE

The Origin of the World

When you think about it, the world is divided into two groups. Those who have children and those who don't. Those who perpetuate the species and those who don't. Those who rely on other people's children to care for them and empty their bins when they are old. Those who have participated in providing the next generation of nurses and cooks, of teachers and refuse collectors. At a huge cost to themselves. But you can never truly understand that if you haven't been there. Some people just prefer a quiet life without children, and who can blame them? Others don't have the choice. It is a brutal fact, which you may not like, but such is the truth. There is really only one story worth telling. The creation of life. Or not. The story that enables humanity to survive.

In the beginning is birth. Carbon from the stars creates a world - the mother, the matrix, the earth. The Origin of the World. That chunky French painter, Gustave Courbet (the one who hated the Communards) well, he was right. You may not like his politics, but on this count he was right, when he put oil to canvas and painted 'The Origin of the World' in 1866. Quite a small painting (46 x 55 centimeters) it could easily be concealed under a *redingote* (a riding coat or frock coat). The woman he painted has not had a Brazilian wax or a carefully

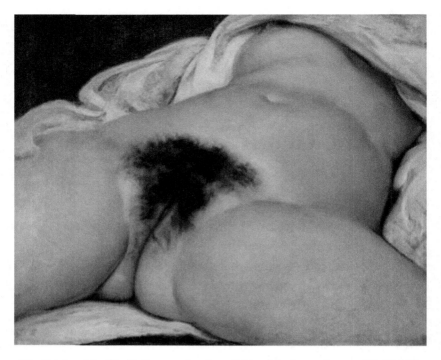

The Origin of the World, Gustave Courbet, 1866, © Musées nationaux (RF 1995 10)

shaved landing strip, but languorously, she exhibits her labia surrounded by a luxuriant bush. She has a nice bosom as well. There is nothing surreal about this painting. It is pure realism, which figures, as Gustave Courbet was the founder of the French Realist School of Art.

Does it make you feel uncomfortable? Voyeur? Some things should be left covered up? Like this headless female body with her most intimate parts exposed, originally for the male gaze only. Carefully composed, Courbet captures the marble like glow of her skin and the carefully draped folds of the fabric. But there is no face watching you from the frame. This is a woman, any woman, every woman. It is what women share, what we all have hidden in our knickers. Revolutionary. It was to be a long time before Lucien Freud painted his female nudes in the 1990s. His beautiful 'Benefits Supervisor Sleeping' (1995) was another shocking painting with a great title.

Only Courbet didn't paint it off the top of his head, off the top of his brush, as a humble tribute to all womankind. No, it was a commissioned piece and its buyer quickly stowed it away, taking it out only occasionally to show to his buddies. And from then on, it was always sold under the table, under the frock coat, till it arrived in the hands of French psychoanalyst-philosopher, Jacques Lacan. Even though he was an upfront psychoanalyst, during his lifetime he too kept it concealed in his study, hidden away behind a removable painted wooden screen. When he died it was handed over to the French State to pay off his death duties and since 1995 it has been hanging in full view, for the whole world to see, in the *Musée d'Orsay* in Paris.

She has no face but as soon as she went on public display in 1995 the only thing the public wanted to know was … who was this woman who so unashamedly revealed her nether regions to Gustave Courbet in 1866? Why did it matter? But it always does. We cannot stand the not knowing. So, academics started working on the enigma and found that Gustave's model was a courtesan, a prostitute. Her story however has a happy ending because Gustave's courtesan posed for many artists who paid her in kind, in paintings, and thanks to these she died a wealthy woman. Astute. Like Bob Dylan who, after sitting for Andy Warhol at The Factory, got up and took a picture of Elvis off the wall. 'That's payment,' he said. Warhol apparently turned a tomato soup red, but didn't run after him to snatch it back.

But really, with this painting, it is the title that is the important part. Courbet could have called it a 'reclining nude'

- and goodness knows there have been plenty of those (like the beautiful, 1930s *'Reclining Pink Nude'* by Chinese émigré Sanyu where there is not a pube in sight.) Or he could have called it something more imaginative - a Viennese oyster, a landing mattress, a female slipper ... or just a plain old Fanny. But he did none of these. He called it *'The Origin of the World'*. And if the Roman Catholic Church had caught wind of it, they would surely have excommunicated him.

Courbet is right. That is precisely what it is. We are all of woman born. Even those who get mixed up in a test tube (though you have to admit that the most efficient, and most fun method of fertilisation is sex.) But after that first spurt of activity, men don't get much of a look-in. Pretty well out of the picture for the next nine months. But all of us have spent nine months inside a

Dogon front door sculpture: Mr and Mrs, outside their home.

woman's body. We all have a feminine side. And just to finish with this question of art and nudity I'd like to say that the Dogon approach to nudity seems to be far healthier - like this amazing carving of male and female, Mr and Mrs outside their front door, meeting all visitors, unabashed, in their simplest apparel. This is a beautiful creation: they are not hiding anything under a frock coat.

Aristotle says women are incomplete men. No penis, you see. But you can forget that penis envy theory. Because if envy there is, it lies in the basement of the male psyche, which cannot get over women's ability to give birth. To create. Creation is of woman born. (True. There may be a few exceptions, like the male seahorse that gets pregnant and gives birth to a herd of little sea-ponies. There's always one who's got to be different).

Where there was nothing, no one, just dried up sperm and browning sanitary pads with that strange fishy smell, one day is transformed by penetration into a life growing in the womb, the matrix, the seat of desire, of pain, of life. A new life, born of an egg and a sperm and growing inside a woman. (The subdivision of gametes they say nowadays - that surprising division of cells, popping up, spreading and growing, like an idea taking shape). Not like the tadpole that grows outside the mother's body in the waters of the pond where the male frog lays its sperm on top of the female's eggs. No penetration of the female. No sex. Nothing happens inside her body and in many respects this is a far more practical solution because the tadpoles can then develop, untrammelled in the muddy waters of the pond, except for the passing predator that might snaffle them up. But you and me, we are hot-blooded mammals and our babies are delivered fully formed, direct from the mother's body.

This is also the fundamental snag. The design fault inherent in the system. What went into the female body was a jet of sperm, like tadpoles ... big heads, small tails, that wriggle up the vagina like salmon, beating their tails, thrashing their way up the ladder. The fittest sperm then penetrates the spongey egg, shedding its tail and together, hand in hand, they bury their way into the wall of the womb, into the heady compost where the cells go into overdrive and divide and multiply, eggstatic. (Couldn't resist that one.)

But the trouble is, they are building their boat inside a garage. Expanding and growing to become a foetus and then a baby (don't ask me when one stops and the other starts, I do not have this competence). And this creation flourishes and is good, until one day, it is just too big for its safe little haven and it has to come out. You have to take the door off the hinges or smash a hole in the wall to get it out. But out it must. If you are lucky, this new life will just flop out, like a seal onto the ice flow, fully formed and viable, once a stranger in a white coat has given it a vicious slap on the back. A taste of what is to come in this brave new world.

There are of course various chapters to this creation story. The Bible tells us so. First there is the tasting of the fruit from the tree of knowledge. Sexual excitement, ecstasy, pleasure. That glorious moment, the meeting of the sperm with the egg, (or the meeting of the egg with the Holy Spirit, but that is more of a rarity). In my case this meeting of an egg with a sperm took place in Marrakech in early 1976, not long after my French boyfriend and I got married. Marriage was what you did in those days if you wanted respectable, regular sex. So, everything was as it should be. Not out of wed-lock. We'd been married in the pretty white chapel of Lathom Park in Lancashire, with the white alms houses standing behind.

But now what preoccupies me, what I really need to tell you, is the story that resurfaces forty years later, with the ransacking of the Vueling moon bags on a flight from Alicante. The tale of the bringing out of my body, that which we had created, my French husband and me.

Before I tell you my story, I should explain that this tale has two narrators: there's the young me, an ingénue who knows nothing, especially nothing about having a baby, and the old me, university lecturer, specialising in what the French call *'civilisation'* (a mixture of history and politics), a bit of a pedant perhaps and definitely obsessed with history. And history nowadays is not easy, the way it used to be when British empiricism ruled the waves and people believed doggedly in the importance of 'hard facts'. All the historian had to do back then, was to pile up these 'hard facts' (that were of course neutral) to arrive at an objective and reliable account of what had really happened.

It is not easy telling your birthing story forty-five years after the event, when everything is happening in your head at once. Linear it is not. And the two narrators get mixed up all the time. What follows is an attempt to sort out these different conversations. So, I crave your indulgence and ask you to bear with ...

CHAPTER TWO

Quantum Entanglement

I didn't know then how this story would finish, but I knew how it had started. In the autumn of 1973, at the *Maître Kanter Taverne* in Bordeaux I encountered a Frenchman. Neck like an ox. Judo black belt. Tanned skin set off against his white cotton shirt. Just returned from Madagascar where he'd been doing his military service in a high school, teaching English. He drove his sister's Peugeot convertible with Gallic dash through the cobbled streets of Bordeaux. Bernard had to get out of Madagascar fast in the summer of '73 because of the *coup d'état* where he'd seen folks in the streets of Antananarivo waving severed arms and legs in the air, above their heads. The French government repatriated him and there were no more visas for foreigners like me to get into Madagascar - where I was supposed to be going to teach in a secondary school. My four-year French degree course at the University of Leicester stipulated that I should spend the third year in France as a language assistant in a Lycée. Only I didn't want to go to France. It seemed a bit tame after a year as an eighteen-year-old VSO volunteer in the bush in Zambia. I wanted to go to French speaking Africa. So, the head of the French department and international specialist on Emile Zola, the lovely Professor Hemmings, had taken my request all the way up to the University Senate and asked them to change the rules for me. And they did. Only now, I couldn't get in to Madagascar because of the coup d'état and I had to find somewhere else to go, quick. One of the set texts for my 'A' levels had been François Mauriac's *'Noeud de Vipères,* 'The Vipers' Nest', a tale set in Bordeaux's twisted vineyards. It wasn't Madagascar, but it was still a long way from the cabbage fields of Ormskirk, where my parents were living at the time. So it was in Bordeaux that I met Bernard. If I couldn't meet him in Madagascar then I would meet him in Bordeaux. It was written in the stars. The second shoe waiting to drop. The shoe that Einstein failed to spot but the folks of Nagasaki knew all about. The other part of your atom. Your matching pair. Quantum entanglement.

I learnt all this from The Open University, the brainchild of Prime Minister Harold Wilson ... whose first constituency was Ormskirk. Among his many achievements as Prime Minister (1964-70 and 1974-76) was the creation of the Open University. (And there were to be many more spooky connections of quantum entanglement with the town of Ormskirk.)

The Open University explained cosmic oneness and quantum entanglement to folks like me, thirsty for knowledge. Explained to us that an action in one place has unforeseeable impacts on other parts of the universe, beyond the bounds of common sense. Me and Bernard. A strange connection. A magical falling together, from Ormskirk to the Bordeaux vineyards. A random process, pulling to the same point, of me meeting him in the *Maître Kanter Taverne* in Bordeaux in 1973. Listen to Professor Brian Cox's poetic explanations of quantum entanglement and the second law of thermo dynamics. And you think you get it. You think you understand it, even when he gets to the end, and smiling, he explains endtropy - which as the name implies, is how it is all going to end. The end of the planet, the end of the universe. Things will fall apart and disintegrate. Because all of these atoms, soul mates or not, are moving further and further apart. But we haven't got there yet. For the moment, we are at the romantic stage.

Before we were married Bernard had been teaching English at the Lycée Moulay Ali Chérif in Ouezzane, a centre for religious teaching, tucked away in the Rif mountains in the north of Morocco. He grew a black curly beard, and the locals called him *el boulhawa,* the respected, 'bearded one' and that made his life a whole lot easier. He came to visit me in Ormskirk in the summer of '74 with his black beard and

squiggly red Moroccan plates on his sable Peugeot car. And one day when he stopped at the lights in Burscough Street, a gang of lads came to bounce on the Peugeot's bonnet and told him to 'eff off. Bloody Palestinian.'

My grandmother didn't like his beard either. When we got married, she told him to shave it off.

'Just do it', she said, 'but don't say I told you, or my granddaughter will never forgive me'. Because I loved his black beard when it got long enough to be soft and downy. So much better than the sandpaper stubble he had

Our wedding, August 1975, at the Chapel of St John the Divine, Lathom Park, Lancashire.

The wedding of my parents, Myra and Ken, St Nicolas Church, Durham, December 1941.

when he shaved twice a day and rubbed my skin red raw. But I couldn't tell my Gran that. He didn't shave it off, but he did trim his beard for our wedding where he looked dashing in his dark suit and pinstriped waistcoat hired from Moss Bros in Liverpool.

Ah and that hat. See that hat. It had to be a hat, large and translucid. Even then I was nostalgic for the 1960s and those heady flower power days. I didn't want a veil, like a vestal virgin, nor a headdress like my mother wore when she married her dashing captain in Durham in 1941. (It was the same headdress that made my niece laugh years later.

'Did Granny go to Disney before she got married?' she asked.

'No?'

'So why is she wearing Minnie Mouse ears?')

Our marriage gave my new husband more points for the French education system, so I was spared Ouezzane and the cows rubbing up against the shutters in the early morning. He got a *'mutation'* and was transferred to the Lycée Hassan II in Marrakech. We rented a flat, rue Ouadi el Mahazine in the European quarter, Gaylees, opposite the tennis club with its orange clay courts and purple bougainvillea. (I can't remember the name of our landlord, which is annoying. He used to drive around in a 1950's sky blue Chevrolet soft top. I can only think of Mr Denysenko, my Greek landlord at Grace Road during my second year at Leicester University.) But like everyone else in Marrakech, we heard the call to prayer five times, day and night, broadcast over the loud speaker.

So, it was here, in Marrakech that my husband's sperm travelled up my birth canal and met my egg. Quantum entanglement: a hidden layer of deep physics that determines our future from the very beginning. The Holy Grail of a universe that is so deeply strange. A connection across space and time, atoms and particles, before we knew for sure.

The doctor took a sample and sent it to a laboratory in Rabat. Then we had to wait ten days while they carried out a clever dosage of Pregnandiol and Phénolsteroïdes. We've still got

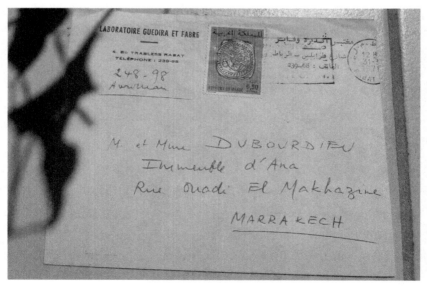

An envelope came bearing the results, March 1976.

the letter and the envelope with the pregnancy test results and remember our hesitation before opening it. Then when we did open it, we didn't know how to interpret the results, and had to wait another few days to see the doctor, who then congratulated us solemnly:

'Parenthood is a long journey. No more alcohol,' said he, who was partial to a drop himself. 'No more *Mouton Rothschild or Gris de Boulaouane,* and no tonic water either,' he said, 'there's quinine in that.' That leaves tea and water.

Then came the months of waiting and not knowing what was to be ...

I thought it was a 'he'. Not because they had scans in those days to check the baby had all its bits in the right place and tell its sex, so you didn't have to buy all of its layette in neutral white. No. I knew because my neighbour on the landing in our block of flats in Marrakech had told me so. She was the one who announced I was pregnant when she found me white, on the landing outside the front door. A splatch of sick on the tiles. Her ululations ricochéd off the concrete

Our baby at 4 months in the womb, in a palm grove full of lilac daisies, in Marrakech, May 1976.

walls. Then she disappeared, returning with a small bottle that she uncorked, making me cry. She rubbed her sharp smelling liquid onto my wrists and into my temples. Forty years later, I still hate the smell of white vinegar. They say it's wonderful for cleaning stains off the tiles, but I can't stand the stuff. But this woman knew a thing or two. She praised Allah for his gift and cleaned up my mess.

Later she praised Allah twice over for his beneficence. We were going to be blessed with a baby, and double blessed, with a boy.

'Of course it's a boy,' she says, 'you are carrying your child high up, just under your heart. Girls,' she says, 'settle lower down, their place is around the stomach and the womb. Boys aspire to higher things'.

We left Marrakech in the middle of May when everyone decided it was too hot to bother any more at the Lycée Hassan II, where the school corridors were filled with sheep and gifts for teachers before the end of term staff meetings. Bernard drove us fast up to Tangiers in our new Peugeot 504. For once we were early, so we waited in the pine forest near the harbour where the pine cones cracked and spat like gun fire in the heat. From Tangiers we got the boat to Sète then stopped off in Bordeaux to see Madame, my mother-in-law, who vaguely said I might stay and have the baby in Bordeaux, if I wanted. We sat out on the terrace at night for the evening meal and the mosquitoes congregated in a cloud above the table. My mother-in-law said she'd never seen any mosquitoes in these parts, no one had ever complained before. But Bordeaux is built on marshland and I was soon covered in itchy red bumps. I bought a sleeveless gingham tent dress to cover my breasts, swollen like airbags.

Have you noticed dear Reader, in all the TV dramas nowadays ... 'Victoria', 'Poldark', as well as all those women

'Calling the Midwife' and giving birth in Poplar (before it became Tower Hamlets)? Have you noticed? They only ever get pregnant from the waist downwards. Their bump starts at the navel and even while they are giving birth, their little breasts lie flatly, chaste against their little chests. Wrong. The first difference you feel, even before you know you're pregnant, is that your breasts are swelling, taught and tingling and suddenly there are things up there on the balcony thrashing about. It is weird to feel your body change and know you are sharing it with someone else. It starts on the inside - the outside only catches up later.

I wandered around the chic streets of Bordeaux peering into pushchairs, looking at bumps of various sizes in elegant maternity dresses. 'I see the girls walk by dressed in their summer clothes, I have to turn my head until my darkness goes'. Appalled and fascinated with new life and serene mothers wheeling their new-borns about. They all seemed to know what they were doing. 'Like a newborn baby it just happens every day'. Well, no, it doesn't. It's a lot more complicated than that. Walking down one of the byways, shading elegant 18th century houses, built on the blood of slaves, behind me comes a scream to curdle your blood and a young lad runs past, cursing and running and hitting his head with the flat of his hand, then yelling some more. And this poor mother comes hurtling after him, 'But Michel,' she shouts, 'be careful of the traffic! Be careful of the cars!'

Then we carried on northwards, sailing from Roscoff to Plymouth where we stopped in a pub for a full English breakfast and I lost half a tooth biting into a slice of toast. Never underestimate English toast. They say you lose one tooth for every child. But finally, we got back home to the north. To Ormskirk, a strange place to want to come back to. Not exactly a place of belonging, Durham is my home.

My upwardly mobile parents had paid for elocution lessons to get rid of my Durham accent, but it was only a superficial success. When I was ten, I was heartbroken when my dad's new job took us away from Durham and over the Pennines. That's why my mother was in Ormskirk and that was the only thing that mattered to me. I came back to Ormskirk for my mother.

You don't choose your birth place any more than you choose your mother. But I got lucky. My mother was wonderful. That doesn't mean we didn't fall out from time to time. But for the long haul she was always there: steady, reassuring, loving. I'm a July birthday, which means that I was always one of the youngest in the class. In infants' school, that makes a difference, because there is practically a year's difference between the oldest and the youngest in the class and I always had trouble with spelling. At age seven, my teacher told my mother that I would never pass the Eleven Plus exam. It was clear, she said, that I didn't have the mental capacity. And my mother, everso politely, told her to get stuffed.

The idea of becoming a mother, was terrifying. I needed all the help I could get. And my mother, in Ormskirk, was where I needed to be. She knew everything about babies (she'd had three of her own and was an infants' school headteacher). Calm and reassuring. It was going to be alright. She sorted out the cot, the mattress, the Maclaren baby detachable carrycot that later turns into a pushchair. Having a baby is an expensive business. There was also the Silver Cross pram, the Rolls Royce of prams, by appointment to Queen Elizabeth II. Though my Mum always said the Queen was a distant mother and definitely not an example. Poor Charles had been sent away to Gordonstoun for morning runs in the mists and cold showers in the Highlands, to make a man out of him. And look how that turned out. Mum said that if they'd been an ordinary family - which obviously they weren't -

they would have been given a social worker. But the high chassis and incredible springs on that Silver Cross pram would be great for negotiating the potholes down Ruff Lane. And the bairn could be parked outside in the garden under the old pear tree to get some fresh air and watch the light dappling through the branches. (But with a net over the top in case the neighbour's cat thinks his little face is just a nice spot to lie on.) A plastic baby bath, a high chair and all of those terry towelling nappies that you had to fold into a triangle and hold together with an enormous safety pin (*une épingle à nourrice* in French - a nanny's safety pin. But which nanny would that be?). The tricky bit was stabbing that pin through all those layers of thick cotton without stabbing into the baby's soft little stomach. What sort of a plan was that?

'Terry towelling can be rough on tender little bums', said Mum, so she went out and found some soft muslin squares to put inside the towelling nappies. A new invention since her time. 'A real step forward,' she said. No one even dreamt of disposable nappies back then. (Though many years later, when disposable nappies were all the rage, an announcement appeared in our municipal magazine, inviting young mothers to discover the advantage of washable nappies. 'Whether for ecological, hygienic or economical reasons,' it said, 'washable nappies are good for baby, good for you (only you have to wash them) and good for the planet. But which ones should you choose? For a mere 60 euros you will get a complete kit of 20 washable nappies, to try out the different models, see which leak the least and work out how you are going to organise all this washing'. It is fun to re-invent the wheel.

My little granny crochets a blanket in soft white wool. 'Has to be white,' she says. 'Can't be sure of the sex', even though she thinks it's going to be a boy. A conclusion that she's reached by pure intuition, far more reliable than her neighbour's 'bread test':

if the pregnant mother craves for the crusts of a loaf, it's going to be a boy. If she craves for all the rest of the loaf - the soft innards - she's going to put on a lot of weight, and it's going to be a girl. Only I preferred crusts for toast and marmite, but would never use them to make sandwiches - so where does that leave me and my babe?

I can't tell even my Mum. Especially not my Mum. I can't tell her about my anxiety. This terrible floating dread, that appeared from the moment that blue envelope arrived. The fear that my baby will be damaged. Wherever I go, the anxiety gets there before me. It is easier just to kept smiling.

A hot summer in Ormskirk. Completely unexpected. Sitting outside by the pond, watching the insects. A mayfly lives for just one day. She mates, reproduces and dies, all in one day. Between four and six in the afternoon, she flies up into the air, just that one time, finds her soul mate, they mate and then satisfactorily fertilised and if she can avoid the waiting birds, she dives back into the water, lays her eggs and dies on the bottom of the pond. That's what you call efficient. No messing about with a long courtship, gestation or labour pains. Someone must have done a time and motion study.

And there's even better than that, I've just found out, looking at the roses in the rose garden, covered in green fly. Aphids. Look closely and you'll see that there's always one big fat aphid who looks as if she's knitting, popping out little aphids, dozens of them, and sticking them to the stems behind her. And they are all daughters. All a genetic copy of herself and all done without sex or fertilisation - parthenogenesis. Virgin birth. No male required. Immaculate conception. No need for any of that messy male sperm. Amazing. Even before they are born, aphids have embryos inside them like Russian dolls and they've been doing this for 200 million years, so no wonder the roses are looking haggard.

Long summer days, 'dog days' they call them, (funny expression that), and with a baby to keep you warm as well, these are the doggiest of dog days, as the roads melt and the smell of tar and feathers wafts up the St Helens' Road in Ormskirk. Perhaps the wood-pigeon's feet got stuck in the tar and he couldn't take off. Now his grey feathers flap whenever a car passes. He'd coo-cooed through the warm nights, indifferent to the old elms and oaks that dried up and tipped over, revealing circles of shallow roots, surprising for such big trees. It's only when a tree falls that you see how tall it was. Fire sweeps through stubble and woodland - a beer bottle, a cigarette thrown out of a car window, nonchalant. Light the blue touch paper and drive on. Heather and moorland roasting the grouse for the glorious 13th. An ancestral form of regeneration, burning the pasture, but you'll have to wait a couple of centuries for the trees to return to their glory.

We go for walks through the lanes of Burscough, where the old Priory used to stand. In the hedgerows and ditches, red admirals and painted ladies flutter over Flanders' poppies, wild marjoram and foxgloves. And when we get back to Ormskirk in the evening, up and down the Southport Road, Derby Street and Railway Road, the inhabitants are out in the sun, stripped to the waist, bellies swinging as they wash and polish Humber Super Snipes, Wolseley Hornets, Ford Poplars, Frog-Eyed Sprites and Singer Gazelles. British Leyland is down the road where my brother works, so there are plenty of Minis parked out on the drives as well. Family treasures on parade.

At night, too hot to sleep, a huge mound rises up in front of me, the belly button pushed inside out, blocking my view. I stroke the bump and it jiggles and jumps. A knee, an elbow, sticks out like someone trying to get out of a jumper. And when the moon is up, the hedgehogs grunt joyous, copulating in the garden.

In the British Isles the weather is a national obsession, and the weather forecast is my favourite TV programme. Reading the stars and the skies and predicting the pleasures and dramas to come. I talk endlessly about the sun and the moon and the weather. And this heat that won't go away is driving folks wild. The snails are shrivelling up, they hate a dry summer and the ants are opening up vents in their heaps to let out the hot air and create a draft. Some inhabitants of this usually damp island feel we are getting too much sun and they emit dire warnings to pale skinned women like me, with a bun in the oven, telling them of the dangers of the 'mask of pregnancy'. This is not a carnival mask, nor the fixed smile you show to the world while your radiator boils over inside. No, this is the mask that the sun and your riotous hormones will paint on your pale face, turning it brown in blotches, hiding the old you that once you knew, hiding the old you beneath. And don't think you'll be able to shed this skin like a snake when the baby is born: it will stay with your forever, brown splodges stamped onto your cheeks and brow, a constant reminder of your pregnancy in the summer of '76.

A pall of petrol fumes hangs over the St Helens' Road, a mirage trembling in the desert as families sit out the August bank holiday in a traffic jam, desperate to get to Southport just to eat an ice cream. Do they know that gravity changes as you move across the world? The more it rains the heavier the pull of gravity. So, in the sweltering heat of '76, families are getting lightheaded, dreaming of paddling pools and ice-creams, while the farmers of Ormskirk are out with their combines sending up plumes of dust, beating the golden fields and making hay while the sun shines, which is does all the time. Only sometimes their blades strike a stone, which lights a spark, which sets the whole harvest on fire. Re-inventing fire, making a blaze the way our ancestors did in the iron age. The world is turning from green to yellow to brown and black. The full moon rises in August with the equinox tides and the blackberries have all shrivelled up.

Did you know that the Eider duck incubates her eggs alone for 40 days? Because her mate has cleared off. In those 40 days in the wilderness, she will lose 40% of her body weight. (I don't have that problem; I seem to be piling it on.) But at the end of August, Bernard has to go back to Morocco, to his pupils. August, die she must. The autumn winds blow chilly and cold and I am left to incubate alone. He drives back down south to Plymouth (avoiding the toast) crossing to Roscoff then on to Bordeaux. Then he will drive through the monotonous Landes forest, the largest man-made forest in Europe, where drivers fall asleep at the wheel and I'm not at his side to prod him awake. If he makes it through the flickering trees he will cross over the Pyrenees, drive the full length of Spain and finally take the ferry from Algeciras to Ceuta, a Spanish enclave on the north African coast.

Bernard is now back in Marrakech and the *Lycée Hassan II,* just down the road from the Mamounia hotel where Winston Churchill painted the palm trees bending in the wind, the Koutoubia Mosque and the Atlas mountains behind. Bernard plays tennis every evening and writes every week, which is nice. I wish I'd kept those letters but we moved around so much, stuff got thrown out.

The next chapter - written mainly by the old me - might seem like a bit of a diversion. But I have an obsession with place and a need to understand my place in the great unfolding of events, that we call history. So, the next chapter is about the place my baby is going to be born - Ormskirk, its stones, and the connections we feel to those who have gone before. When a baby comes into the world, we know we are part of something bigger. That we are not alone. That we carry history in our bones and search to understand the part we have been given

Some time
Sooner or later
we all have a rendezvous
The crossing of tracks, the meeting of paths
Me becomes us
one night,
where the
Liverpool and Southport,
Wigan and Preston,
Roads collide
in
The old Norse town
of
Ormskirk

But if this gets too annoying, you can just skip the next chapter and move on to the more interesting bits, mostly written by the young me, when I finally reach the old workhouse hospital, down the Wigan Road in Ormskirk. And a new life is born.

You will also find that there are some other interspersed interludes written by the old me. These I have put in italics, should you wish to ignore them as well.

CHAPTER 3

Ormskirk

As we walk through the streets of Ormskirk, we take a circuitous route to the old workhouse hospital, which is the centre of what turns out to be, a real-life horror story. Sneak up on it. Come at it from a tangent. You don't have to, if you don't want. But it would be nice to have the company.

Restless and anxious, pushing my bump in front of me, through the streets of Ormskirk, avoiding the patches of melted tarmac and clutching my Air France sick bag. I don't usually need it. It's just moral support, really. Thursday. I forgot it's Thursday, market day, and there's a nauseous smell of fish. Brought in fresh in the early morning from Iceland and Fleetwood, now the ice is melting and fish skins and scales are shining in the gutter. Did I tell you that Ormskirk is at the junction of the main roads to Liverpool, Preston and Wigan? The local guide book says there have been 'weekly markets here since the 13th century where farmers, cottagers, cow keepers and fishmongers trade their goods.'

Let's get away from the smell and go up to the church to find some shade. This is the church where my sister got wed in 1970 but I wasn't there - I was hitching-hiking my way back from Zambia, via Rhodesia and South Africa, with a friend. But that was another life.

When you're pregnant, you are sensitive to the ghosts

and souls that surround you. We are fragments of the past: fish scales and ferns, hunter gatherers, bronze age farmers, Romans, Norsemen and Dane law. Then comes William, the Plantagenets, the Tudors, the Stuarts, the Hanoverians and Victoria. They all passed through these parts. You might not see them, but your baby hears them.

Orme's kirk: its tower and steeple at the very same end.

Your guide for today, through the streets of Ormskirk, is the older me, the would-be historian:

The first remarkable thing about Ormskirk is that it has the only church in the whole of the country with both a tower and a steeple. Now those of you who are members of the National Trust will know that there are two churches in Wiltshire with this same peculiarity (both tower and steeple) ... however dear Reader, before you start shouting me down, I would like to point out that what makes Ormskirk's church so completely and utterly unique is the fact that both its tower and its steeple are situated at the very same end of the very same edifice, giving this church a somewhat queasy feel.

Lopsided. Leaning to the left. And I'm not saying that because Harold Wilson, was one time MP for Ormskirk, but you already know that. It was his first seat in Parliament and the first time marks you forever. On becoming Prime Minister in 1964, a journalist asked him as he was leaving for Buckingham Palace to meet the Queen: 'Do you feel like a Prime Minister Harold?'

'Quite honestly', he replied, 'I feel like a drink.'

It's a bit of a climb up to the church, but here we are, outside the oldest building in the old market town of Ormskirk, named after the old Norseman, Orme (meaning 'sea serpent' or 'dragon' in old Norse) and Kirkja, the kirk. Orme built his kirk on this sandy outcrop, after he ran his longboat aground some miles away in the Mersey estuary. The name 'Mersey' you might like to know, means 'frontier' or 'border', because on the other side of the Mersey lies the great unknown, The North.)

Orme then decided enough was enough. This time he wasn't going to rape and pillage and carry his treasure and his slaves all the way back to Norse-land-Norway. He would throw his two-handed battle-axe and Viking shield into the muddy waters of the Mersey and settle down on this rich and fertile land, known even then for its fat pigs and cabbages. Orme understood that only land brings true power and prestige. (Although he also had a huge treasure trove and legend has it that he buried his hoard somewhere in these parts. But as yet, no plough has ever turned it up and Ormskirk's metal detectors still live in hope). Orme, the Norseman, also brought with him useful new skills, such as sharply shaven Nordic hairstyles and the technique of smoking meat and fish over oak chips. (Thank Orme when you next have a slice of smoked salmon.) But Orme was not on his own, he did not come by himself. He was accompanied by his two sisters, squabbling siblings, that he hadn't managed to shake off on the Mersey mudflats. And his two sisters (whose names we do not know, but they were probably anglicised anyway), his two sisters then persuaded Orme that if he wanted to get along with the hairy peoples of these parts (who had yet to discover Orme's razor blades), then it would be prudent to give up Thor and Odin and the promise of all those virgins in Valhalla, and convert to the new cult of Christianity which was all the rage. For Orme was getting old - probably approaching thirty. Thus, this barbaric raider gave up his Norse ways and started to build his kirk to the new Christian God. But still his sisters could not agree. The elder declared she wanted a thrusting tower, while the younger believed an elegant spire, piercing the clouds and drawing the eye heavenward would be more in keeping with the new Christian aesthetic. So in his newfound desire for reconciliation and a quiet life, Orme built a kirk with a tower and a steeple, taking care to place both tower and steeple at the very same end of the very same structure, thus putting paid to all discussions over who would have the better view over the fertile lands of Ormskirk. Well, that at least is what legend tells us. You can take it or leave it. As you please.

It is, however, also interesting to note that 'Orme' can be translated from the old Norse, by the term 'worm' - which of course all medieval scholars will tell you has throbbing phallic significance, as we can see in the painting below of the Laidley Worm of Spindlestone Heugh. The

The Laidley Worm of Spindlestone Heugh, 1881, by Walter Crane, R.W.S., Courtesy of Fine Art Photographs, London.

young maiden, with no clothes on (no pubes either), looks adoringly at the muscular knight (huge sword, Viking helmet and spurs) who is saving her from the enormous worm ... though we may doubt the knight's chivalric intentions, as his own chain 'male' morphs alarmingly into the shining silver of the writhing serpent.

Be honest. You don't get more erotic than that, with the fully clad knight, rescuing the naked maiden (flowing locks, pert nipples) from the Worm ...which is enormous.

We have established that the name Orme means worm, but to dub him 'Orme the Dick' might be a bit over the top. Though it is true that 'Orme the Dick' is probably not a soubriquet that the nubile young academics of the Open University on BBC4 would shun. You've got to make history (or more often, her-story .... grrr) sexy they say. Didn't the serpent, the worm, tempt our mother Eve and make her eat of ... well, what exactly? Not an apple, nor a pear, none of that. The worm beguiled Eve with a pomegranate, that glorious golden fruit that grew in abundance in the gardens of Persia. A symbol of fertility if ever there was one, with all those blood red seeds. The Koran says every pomegranate contains one seed that comes from paradise. The difficulty is knowing which one.

But we must press on. Orme the sea serpent, Orme the worm, Orme the dick - whatever happened to courtly love? Orme and his decision to build both a tower and a spire, which personally I do not believe was a transgressive incestuous act to pleasure both his sisters. But it is this act, which you are free to interpret as you will, (especially if you are an Open University academic) - this very act of placing a tower and a steeple at the very same end of the very same building gives a queasy, uneasy feel to Orme's kirk today as we stare up at it. Unbalanced. Unstable.

It makes my younger self wobble on the edge of its sandy outcrop. Makes her feel sick. Pass her that moon bag. Though it is true that this queasiness may also be due to a problem with our cervical vertebrae that lock together as we get older, and which is unfortunately common among members of the National Trust. (I said cervical vertebrae. The vertebrae of the neck, immediately below the skull. which can cause cervical vertigo, fatigue. I am not for the moment talking about the cervix, the neck of the womb. We will get there soon enough).

Having pondered this unsettling peculiarity of Orme's kirk, we will now enter the church, which will allow my younger self some shade. Feels almost damp. And by entering the Parish Church of both Saint Peter and Saint Paul we now leave behind Orme the Viking and jump ahead to the seventeenth century where we will notice on the walls, the many connections with the Earls of Derby and the Stanley family - who are one and the same, though this may not be obvious. For Derby, as you all know, is to be found in Derbyshire, a considerable distance from Ormskirk where we are today, in Lancashire.

If we proceed to the Derby Chapel, we will find members of the Stanley family, including the very first Earl of Derby. Now Stanley got to be the Earl of Derby, because he was said to be a 'king maker'. Whichever side he chose on the Battle field of Bosworth in 1485 (which pitched King Richard III, against Henry Tudor, Duke of Richmond.) whichever side he chose, would become king. Stanley hesitated, weighing up which side would be most advantageous for him and his family. Two lines at the end of Shakespeare's Richard III say it all:

King Richard III: *"What says Lord Stanley? Will he bring his power?"*

Messenger: *"My Lord, he doth deny to come."*

A good decision, because Henry Tudor then created this title of Earl of Derby for Stanley, after he'd switched allegiance from the last Plantagenet King, Richard III. (And I bet you don't know how the Plantagenets got their name. It's logical enough when you think about it. The founding father of the Plantagenet dynasty (whose name escapes me for the moment), apparently enjoyed gardening and improving the landscape and spent much of his time à planter genêts, that is to say planting broom bushes - those pretty yellow flowers that bloom on the heath, providing cover for the game birds that he enjoyed hunting. So, Plant à Genêts, *became Plantagenets. Not a lot of people know that, as Franky Howard used to say.)*

For the Stanleys, switching sides was a canny move which we now know caused Richard III to lose his crown in a carpark in Leicester (which is neither in Lancashire nor Derbyshire). Richard III staggered around the field in Bosworth looking for a horse and his friends, till Stanley and Henry Tudor's lads fell upon him and buried him in a ditch, filling his mouth with dirt while he was still breathing, poor man. Stanley and the Tudors said he wasn't a true king but an evil hunchback, because in those days your physical appearance was believed to reveal your inner self, so of course he must have killed those two little princes in the tower. Which was not true. Richard III was maligned by historians, as well as by William Shakespeare, who did a lot to perpetuate the myth. However today, some scholars will tell you that in fact Shakespeare wasn't Shakespeare at all. Shakespeare was in fact none other than the VIth Earl of Stanley ... which would be wonderful if it were true, as it would tie in very nicely with our tale.

Anyway, when archaeologists found this skeleton in Leicester with a curved spine (scoliosis like Richard's which had developed after his birth), there was great excitement. Careful examination of the remains further revealed that Richard III had undergone the ritual humiliation of having a sword thrust up through his buttocks. And for 530 years Richard lay in an unmarked grave in down-town Leicester. It is heart-warming to note that on the 26th of March 2015, Richard III was buried with the pomp and circumstance due to a king, in Leicester Cathedral, in a coffin made by a Canadian cabinet maker, who is in fact his great-great-great-great nephew. Even after all those years, family counts. Our history is what we carry around with us and pass on to the next generation.

Some of the earth that had covered Richard's body was also buried in a time capsule within the city walls of York, which would have become England's capital, had Richard III, the last Plantagenet king, survived. We are all linked. We are all part of something bigger.

As well as the title of Earl of Derby, Henry Tudor showered great wealth on the Stanley family, which prompted the first earl's son, Thomas (2nd Earl of Derby) to build the beautiful Lathom park chapel (consecrated in 1500) which later, in 1975 was the place I married my handsome Frenchman. I told you. We are all inter-connected. But you must also appreciate that Ormskirk has long been a treacherous place .... a place where people hedge their fields and hedge their bets, turn their coats and sharpen their knives.

In this same Derby chapel, situated in Orme's kirk, we also find the mortal remains of the seventh Earl of Derby, the Royalist James Stanley, beheaded at the end of a very uncivil war, by Cromwell in 1651. You will remember that George Orwell (a man of many parts and different names) on his way to Wigan Pier, tells us that it is the victor who gets to write the history. He also gets the pleasure of chopping off the heads of his enemies. For in this very place, in Ormskirk's Derby chapel, we find buried in a coffin, the headless trunk of the seventh earl of Derby, who sleeps uneasy here in Lancashire, forever detached from his head, which is also buried here, in a separate casket, beside his truncated body. And on All Hallows' Eve, when the moon rises above the tower and the steeple, and the branches scrape their long fingernails down the windows of the kirk, the locals tell you that there is a squeaking and scratching that chills your blood, like the squeaking and scratching of an army of rats on the march, as the headless body of the seventh earl drags his head in a casket behind him. That, dear Reader, is what folklore tells us. It's up to you to decide what credence, or not, you can afford it.

However, on a more personal and factually verifiable note, your old narrator here would like to point out that it was, to this very same church, packed with this ghoulish history, that she herself came in the dark month of November 1976, tainted with the original female sin. She had to be 'churched' once she had been delivered of a child in the old workhouse hospital of Ormskirk.

We are all part of this great historical unfolding. Orme, Cromwell, the earls of Derby, your narrator(s). And 'churching' as some of our older readers will know, consists in the symbolic cleansing of a mother when the dirty business of childbirth is over. Go forth and multiply sayeth the Lord. But this has always been a messy business for the descendants of Eve. And when it is all over, when the woman has been through the travails of labour, when the large fruit in her womb has been plucked out, then the female of the species has to come to church to prove that she can stand up on her own, unassisted. No disgraceful bodily fluids running down her legs. To prove that she is fit once more, to be received into polite society. She can be invited into your house and trusted not to leave ugly brown stains on your cushions and carpets. And once 'churched', the church will then allow her to present her child for baptism. (No churching, no baptism). The jovial Irish priest in situ *in Ormskirk when my time had come, the very Reverend Roberts, assured me that this was the thing to do. In 1975 he had officiated at our wedding at Lathom Park Chapel. You remember that Lathom Park House had been a royalist stronghold belonging to the VIIth Earl of Derby (before he lost his head), but after a long and bloody siege by Cromwell's men, it was completely destroyed. Too ostentatious for Cromwell. They were having too much fun.*

But Reverend Roberts had his doubts about my future husband Bernard, with his curly hair and rampant black beard. A Frenchman living in Morocco. And when the papers didn't arrive from the French Embassy in Casablanca, saying the bans had been read and there was no opposition to our union, the Reverend's suspicions increased. He drew my father aside and asked if he was sure Bernard wasn't a Mohammedan with three wives back in Morocco?

'Well,' said my dad, 'as far as I know Bernard is a bachelor. He was christened a Catholic but never went to his first communion in Bordeaux because he got expelled from the catechism classes for throwing snowballs at Monsieur le Curé.'

'And they have snow now do they? In Bordeaux? Amongst all them vineyards?' Came the reply from the sceptical priest.

Bernard kept ringing the French Embassy to make sure they had indeed published the bans and were going to send the papers. But he could get no answer, till late one afternoon, someone picked up the phone. It was the concierge, *who told him it was August. What was he thinking? Bernard said the chapel was booked, the flowers were ordered, the dress had been made, he needed those papers. But there was no one at the Embassy. Everyone was at the beach. He couldn't be French if he didn't know what it was like in August. Everyone goes to the beach in August. Voices were raised.*

'Oh well', said the caretaker, 'if you insist. If it's really urgent, then you can call around tomorrow and see for yourself.'

Bernard glared at the phone and hung up. 'I'll strangle them

Lathom Park Chapel of St John The Divine, by Peter Andrew, with its eight almshouses. Together they were intended as a hospice, a haven for the sick and the injured, and hopefully a place to die in peace.

all,' he said. Because that was how he had won most of his judo competitions.

Surprisingly perhaps, Cromwell did not tear down Lathom Park Chapel nor its Alms houses. They are still there today and well worth a visit ... and not just because your narrator got married there. If you do go, look out for the bullet holes left by Cromwell's muskets as they tore into the beautifully carved oak choir screen.

The papers finally turned up and the Reverend Roberts came to our wedding reception at Edge Hill College of Higher Education, and we still treasure the six cut-glass sherry glasses that he presented to us on that occasion. Edge Hill College of Higher Education has since become Edge Hill University, though perhaps not many people have heard of it. It's another one of those misplaced places, isn't it? Edge Hill? Edge Hill is in Warwickshire on the border with Oxfordshire. The site of the first battle of the English civil war in 1642. A victory for the Royalists, but we all know that wouldn't last.

Though weddings may still be in vogue, the custom of 'churching' a mother after childbirth does seem to have fallen from use. I cannot remember exactly what it entailed. Poor banished children of Eve. I wasn't stripped and waterboarded. I suppose I was bespattered with Holy water and blessed. But there is no commemorative plaque affixed to the wall of Orme's Kirk to mark this act of paternalist oppression, though someone might suggest it to the Parish Council.

In more recent times, and to the best of my knowledge, Ormskirk has only been in the news twice: once to warn parents to keep a more watchful eye on their children after razor blades (of the type first introduced by Orme?) were found in one of Ormskirk's parks, planted in the wooden panels down the side of the children's slide. Wafer thin steel and razor sharp, ready to slice up the tender flesh of innocents. A whoosh down the slide in a little summer dress that leaves a trail of bright red blood. Blood running along the silver steel that has been burnished by many little bottoms over generations. Little ones having fun. What sick mind would do such a thing? Someone wanting to leave his mark? Get rid of the kids from the park, leave the dealers free to deal in peace? Or just disciples of Cromwell perhaps? No pleasure, we're Puritan.

Parents in Ormskirk are exhorted to keep their eyes open and their guard up, though the report does not say which of Ormskirk's parks was

Postcard 1903: 'Our Lads Returning from the Boer War'

concerned. Let's get out of this church and move on. Was it the park dedicated to Victoria-Imperatrix-Regina, impregnated many times by Albert before he passed on to Valhalla?

Ormskirk is a Victorian town and Victoria Park contains statues to the heroes of the Crimea and the Boer Wars. Many of these heroes were mutilated by the knives and the muskets and yes, the canon to the right of them and the canon to the left of them that volleyed and thundered. But many were also maimed and mutilated by British surgeons, long before the NHS took over. There were no x-rays in those days. Marie Curie hadn't made it out to the Cape of Good Hope where a lot of the injured heroes didn't need amputations but got them anyway. Men with broken ankles were getting their legs amputated. It was easier and cleaner that way, said the surgeons.

Perhaps these heroes passed through Victoria's pleasant park, where we stand now, and looked upon the statues erected to their glory, on their way to Ormskirk's Workhouse just down the road, that we will be visiting shortly.

The other memorable fact about Ormskirk in recent times, is that it is the start, or the finish, depending on which end you are coming from, of the Ormskirk to Preston railway line.

The Ormskirk to Preston railway line was built in the mid nineteenth century, at the peak of the Victorian era when trains were the pride of Britain and her industrial revolution. These train lines were the arteries of the country - some leading to the heart, others to the extremities. The line that

Ormskirk's Victorian railway station

goes from Ormskirk to Preston is undoubtedly one of the extremities and today it is renowned for being the worst line in the whole of the country. Now in these days of truly appalling rail transportation that is quite a record. Well done, Ormskirk. Top of the heap for something. And let's not forget Preston (where Cromwell, vastly outnumbered by a huge Cavalier army, won a surprising victory. 'This,' said Cromwell, 'was proof that God - with whom he had a close personal relationship - well, God was on his side'). Preston later became a proletarian industrial centre, famous in the second world war when Uncle Sam sent his segregated battalions to fight for freedom against racism, fascism and the third Reich. But Uncle Sam believed it wasn't a good thing for the black and the white GIs to meet up, even on leave. The Americans called it 'furlough' (funny word that) and it was advisable to keep the blacks and the whites separated, even on 'furlough'. If the white GIs from the old south spotted a black GI with a white fiancée, however consenting she may have been, then all hell broke loose. It was decided to send the white GIs to the balmy seaside resort of Southport ... though because the British Isles are now tipping to the east, the sea never comes in and remains parked about a mile away from the beach. So, find yourself a donkey if you want to go for a paddle in Southport. This is not always advisable however, as for many years, balls of raw sewage were washed up on this shoreline as the Victorians tipped their faecal matter, untreated, into the sea. Because of this unhygienic situation and the raw sewage rolling around on these sands, the European Union declassified them, refusing to call them beaches at all, as they were simply not fit for purpose. Naturally this infuriated the locals who never wondered why they contracted so many ear, nose and throat infections, as well as acute diarrhoea if they ever managed to take a dip. They vented their spleen on the common market. Whistle blowers are never popular.

Be that as it may, the white GIs were sent to Southport. (How many of them contracted e-coli related diseases before they were shipped out to the cleaner waters of France, to be gunned down on Normandy's beaches in June 1944, we will never know, unless some Open University professor delves into that archive.)

But apart from this minor sewage inconvenience, Southport has always been a genteel Victorian seaside resort. Visit the Prince of Wales Hotel with its Three Feathers Bar and world-famous cocktails. The Prince of Wales, Edward the VIIth (like the VIIth Earl of Derby have you noticed? Seven.) The Prince of Wales was a frequent visitor to Southport and he would generally stop on his way there to enjoy Ormskirk's world famous ginger bread. Another frequent visitor was Napoleon the 3rd. (There we are again - three. Like Richard III, and the third Reich). For Napoleon the 3rd, Napoleon Bonaparte's nephew and his oh-so-elegant wife the Princess Eugénie were exiled to England for some time. (And that's another interesting fact, which perhaps I should put into a footnote, but my editor tells me people never read footnotes.) In 1870, when the English expected Napoleon's nephew to launch an invasion on the British south coast and were desperately reinforcing their battlements, Napoleon III was curiously defeated by the dashing Prussians who arrived in Paris and were always in a hurry to get served in the taverns of Montmartre. 'Bistro! Bistro!' ('Quick, Quick') they would shout ... which gave birth to the now famous Bistros of Paris). Anyway, the defeated Napoleon III asked for asylum in Britain, which was granted after some discussion and the support of Queen Victoria who had a soft spot for Napoleon's nephew. Later when he returned to France and created France's Second Empire, it was to Southport with its elegant boulevards that he turned for inspiration. Napoleon III ordered Baron Haussmann to tear down the meandering medieval streets of Paris and create her splendid wide boulevards that we know today. Boulevards wide enough for a battalion of hussars to charge down, riding abreast, demolishing the barricades and trampling protesters under foot. (You've seen Les Misérables, you know what I am talking about.) Napoleon was also inspired by Southport's parks and green spaces, public benches and elegant street lamps, which are such a signature of Paris today. All thanks to Southport. Not a lot of people know that. Napoleon III's beautiful wife Eugénie on the other hand, went on to create other classy seaside resorts (minus the sewage problems we hope) like Biarritz and Dinard.

But we digress. The white GIs stationed in the north west were sent to the elegant seaside Southport, while the black GIs went to Preston, a town of satanic mills and black smoke. Perhaps they even took the train. But it is the Ormskirk to Preston railway line that in 2018 claimed the number one slot as the worst railway line in the whole of the country. And that takes some doing. Two thirds of the trains are late, cancelled, or they just disappear into the fog and mists that rise from the fields and polders of Ormskirk.

Is that all there is to Ormskirk today? Some little prankster trying to slice up your kid for fun? Not getting to work on time? Telling your boss over and over it's the Ormskirk to Preston train service the problem. He may be sympathetic for a while, but then he'll tell you to bugger global warming and buy a car.

We are now approaching the statue erected to commemorate another first earl. The first earl of Beaconsfield. (There is a pattern emerging here isn't there? One, three, seven. Remember those numbers).

Of course, the first Earl of Beaconsfield is better known as Disraeli, Benjamin Disraeli. Though Ormskirk may have been founded by Vikings, dear Reader, it is a town today that is dominated by another V. V for Victoria.

Benjamin Disraeli was one of Victoria's favourite Prime Ministers, and she got through a good few... But Benjamin Disraeli was different from the rest - he was the grandson of a Jew who came from Venice, and like Orme he converted to Christianity. Benjamin then became the champion of the Anglican Church, the Monarchy and ... the British Empire, because it was Benjamin Disraeli that proclaimed Queen Victoria Empress of India (though she never set her dainty little foot out there. Size three I believe. Three again.). That was in 1876. The creation of the glorious British Empire on which the sun never set. But history is a convoluted narration and we will not open the debate to determine who paid to erect that statue of Disraeli, why they felt it necessary to revere such a man, and whether he should now be pulled down. He wasn't there in Orme's time. Perhaps he replaced the stone phallus the Vikings erected at the entrance to all their settlements to bring good fortune and ward off the evil eye. The Victorians didn't go in much for phallic symbols, but they loved statues.

Perhaps Disraeli should now be rehoused in a museum? Liverpool perhaps. The Tate Gallery? Built with the money from sugar and slaves. We haven't time for such reflections, but only note, that precisely one century later, in 1976, another Benjamin was waiting to be brought into this world. Uncanny.

There is also another fact, dear Reader, that you may like to kick around. You who are thirsty for

Statue of Benjamin Disraeli, first earl of Beaconsfield

history and anxious to understand your place therein. You who take inspiration from your ancestors and those who have gone before. For there is a fact, an occult, hidden fact that very few people know about Victoria Imperatrix Regina. Repressed Empress Queen, buttoned up to the neck, draped with jet black jewellery from Whitby, she who covered up the legs of her piano in black pantaloons so she would not be reminded of the well-rounded calves and vigorous thighs that she had lost with the departure of her lusty German Prince ... for like everyone else, Victoria Regina was not what she seemed. Indeed, underneath the draped black exterior, underneath, down-below, Victoria Regina wore crotchless knickers. Precisely. Not many people know that. Like something out of an Anne Summers catalogue.

Victoria was the most famous woman in the world at the time, (way ahead of Sarah Bernhardt who did her best to catch up by sleeping in a coffin and keeping a cheetah). Victoria too had a passionate sex life. She loved her lusty German lord, but could have done without all the little shrimps that kept popping out. Nine in eighteen years. And she was tiny, Victoria. She loved dancing, loved bright colours and jewellery and she loved sex. But nobody mentioned

Victorian coins

that. Although Victoria and the Victorians did allow themselves to give polite expression to their erotic feelings through their love of scantily attired, sprites, fairies and water spirits, swept along on waves of lust.

However, when Victoria's German Prince died in 1861 she took on the widow's weeds and dragged the whole nation down with her. Black is black. Until she, in her turn, died 40 years later on the Isle of Wight.

We too are part of this great historical unfolding: Orme, Victoria, Anne Summers. We too are trying to find our place in this story.

Arthur Rackham plate for 'Undine', an early German romance, of a water spirit who marries a knight named Huldebrand.

We have nearly arrived at the old workhouse which subsequently became Ormskirk and District General Hospital. It is still to be found on the Road to Wigan where we are now. Wigan is interesting of course, because at the time George Orwell wrote his famous Road to Wigan Pier, *it was like the Swiss Navy. It didn't have one. Wigan didn't have a pier. That was the joke. But since then, in a desperate attempt to pull in the tourists I suppose, Wigan has now built a pier, thus destroying Eric Blair's little joke.*

So here we are then, in front of the black stone walls of the old workhouse, today known as Ormskirk's General Hospital. If you look it up, you will see that they describe it as an 'acute' hospital. I don't know what that means, but I suspect it was always so. The workhouse was the most redoubtable of all Victorian institutions, where the pauper had to be grateful for what he was given and punished if ever he dared complain. Ask Oliver Twist.

'Please sir, can I have some more?' 'No boy. You cannot. And I will flog you for asking'.

As you see, the workhouse buildings of Ormskirk are little changed. Built in the early 1850s, there were imbecile wards, vagrants' wards, children's wards and the general hospital wards. The paupers and tramps would pay for a night's board with the sweat of their brow and their hard labour. This is crusty Victorian Mudfog. You don't want the poor and the needy getting comfortable. The poorhouse is the workhouse. But this workhouse also had a maternity ward, because the needy and the poor kept on multiplying ... as well as Victoria of course, with her crotchless knickers and royal vagina that expelled nine babes. The rich get richer and the poor get babies. Victoria in fact got both. She just loved sex with her handsome Prince. But she was also a woman and a mother who felt the searing pain of pushing a child out of her entrails. Though it was still better to be born a toff, than a ragamuffin in the workhouse. Better to be of royal lineage and married off into the royal houses of Europe (which explains how Philip of Greece, husband to Elizabeth II, was also her cousin. But that is what did for the Habsburgs ... all that in-breeding). It is however true that Victoria Regina was a mother on a large scale, and she wasn't even Catholic. There was just no reliable contraception at the time. As a young bride she tried jumping up and down ten times after lusty intercourse with Albert, trying to stop any fertilised egg latching onto the wall of her womb. Not so repressed after all. Gusset-less knickers and nine children.

Days scroll past, one by one, slowly they turn into history. I can't sleep at night. I do not know what the future holds for me and my baby. How he has been harmed. Which of his eyes, his arms, his legs, fingers or toes will be missing. I was carrying another being inside of me. Another life. But I knew him. We knew each other. Just I didn't know what I'd done to him.

Wrapped around each other. Snug. I wanted that to last. I think he did too. The comfort, the safety, the companionship. But I also needed to know...

CHAPTER 4

The Workhouse

The workhouse impregnates and blackens our story.

I first came to the old workhouse, which became Ormskirk and District General Hospital, in the summer of 1971 when I applied for a job, and got assigned to what used to be the 'Imbecile wards', working as a 'lunatic attendant'.

As a student I wanted to earn money to buy my first car. *A Hillman Imp.* 'Hillman Limp' my brother called it. Brown. I don't know if it was cheaper that colour. I don't think so. I remember having a brown duvet cover in my room in halls at Leicester University (long before they found Richard in the carpark). In 1971 brown was trendy - but you have to say 'on trend' now, don't you? And my brown *Hillman Imp* was a funny contraption. It had the gear box in the boot. Not that I noticed. My brother pointed this out.

'Like trying to swot a fly with a broom,' he said, 'changing gear.' (He worked at British Leyland so he knew about these things). But you always remember your first car, don't you? It spells freedom and I could drive back from Leicester to Ormskirk with the radio balanced on the passenger seat blasting out Tony Blackburn on Radio1 (though I had to remember not to break too hard or the radio would crash to the floor). The Hillman worked most of the time, except when the battery corroded and overflowed with water, so I took it back to the garage, Charlie's, at the bottom of St Helen's Road.

'This battery is making water' I said.

'Bleedin' miracle', says Charlie. 'Holy water is it? Bleedin wimin drivers... Go on. Own up. You overfilled the battery'.

I suppose it was a compliment really. I didn't know you had to put water into a battery.

Anyway in the summer of '71, I applied for a temporary job at Ormskirk and District General Hospital, in the buildings of the old workhouse. They gave me a white coat with a white canvas belt and big shiny buckle, and a navy-blue cloak with a flashy red lining. Very Florence Nightingale. And they sent me to work in the psychiatric (formerly lunatic) ward - only it wasn't just psychiatric. When there weren't enough beds, they put the geriatric cases in there as well. After a while these patients got bed sores on their heels from the rubbing of the rough cotton sheets. One patient was put in there after she'd had a breast removed. I was told to accompany the doctor while he examined her. I stood well back by the door.

'Come here young woman,' said the doctor and I gaped at the one breast, all alone without its partner, where there was now just a ragged scar. I didn't know that was possible. Chopping off a breast. Hacking it out. I wasn't even a psychology student. Only first year French. Some days we were all locked up in the psychiatric ward together because some of the inmates tried to escape, while others would just wander off if they were left unattended. One woman was found miles away walking through the Mersey Tunnel. She said she wanted to get to the other side.

She said she had to see her sister. It turned out her sister was long since dead but the police closed the tunnel for 3 hours. Most inconsiderate someone told her. Only thinking of yourself.

The matron didn't know what to make of me and wasn't best pleased to have a first year French student foisted on her. It was a new venture, a tentative modernisation by the Board of Governors and a young psychiatrist, trying to bring fresh air into Ormskirk's lunatic ward: a collection of clueless students to help out with the sick, the tortured and the miss-fits. The vicar's son also got a summer job there and we would meet up in the cafeteria to exchange notes and try and make sense of it, over milky coffee and Battenberg cake. And also, to take the weight off our feet. It was hard on your feet. I'd been told to buy a pair of sensible black shoes, but didn't want to shell out for leather, so bought plastic, which made my feet hot and sweaty and perfumed the locker I'd been given to store my uniform overnight.

The vicar's son was also a bell ringer and we even stepped out together one night, up the bell tower in Orme's church. He explained that the bells had come from Burscough Priory when Henry VIII had demolished the monasteries, and they built the tower to house them (big disappointment, as this puts paid to the alternative theory of Orme's squabbling sisters.)

Anyway, every morning the young psychiatrist would arrive at the old workhouse in his battered Austin minivan, with a big black dog in the back. Some days when the cabbages were ripe and rotting in the fields of Ormskirk, he turned up wearing his dad's old gas mask. At the lunch break he would get his black dog out of the minivan, attach him to a washing line and take him for an airing in the neatly laid out grounds of the workhouse. The dog would sniff around the trees, wrapping his washing line round and around the trunks with the young psychiatrist in tow.

When I went to get paid at the end of the first week the woman behind the desk glared at me. 'Who d'you think you are anyway?' she said, 'running around. Like that. In a lab coat. All in white. That is no uniform. That is no uniform that I recognise. And don't you dare come in here. Don't you dare come in here, into my presence, ever again, without your cape on.'

Depression is common and it's not all post-natal - though as I found out later, if you have your baby in this particular workhouse-hospital you stood a good chance of catching it. But there were other reasons for depression. Other reasons to get stuck in the polders of Ormskirk, unable to find a way out. The inmates were all different: there was a skeletal fifteen-year-old who looked like she was seven or eight. She would hide her sick in her hot-water bottle that I had to find, under the bed or in her locker, but usually the smell was a dead give-away. There was a shy woman, gentle and sweet who came with her exercise book filled with words and phrases scribbled in different coloured inks, rambling over the pages.

'See,' she says. 'You cannot escape your past. But you know that don't you? If only I could find a publisher. It might help some other body else to know this.'

And this other woman. Glamorous like a film star. Huge blue eyes, framed with amazing black lashes and wavy black hair. But she was a Catholic and no matter how many times she went to confession she could not forgive herself for having had an affair with a dashing captain of industry, a friend of her husband. She was a bad mother. A bad wife. A bad person. And she couldn't be told otherwise. They'd given her anti-depressants, but she saved them all up and took them in one go. 'Think of your children,' they said, 'they need you, they love you.' But she was beyond that. So, her husband had her 'sectioned' - forcefully interned, against her will, under section whatever of the Mental Health Act. He never knew what he would find when he came home at night. He was living off his nerves, poor man. Which just added to her guilt. Her husband brought her to the old workhouse in Ormskirk where they locked her up in the psychiatric ward and gave her ECT treatment. Electric Convulsive Therapy. That'll shift depression when nothing else will, get rid of those obsessive, destructive thoughts. Scramble them. Move them around. Take her electric currents out of their usual circuits and burn a new path. Re-wire her synapses. They told me to sit with her while she came round in the recovery room after the ECT, hold her hand and get her to talk while I tried not to stare at the red marks on her temples. Raised welts. Circles in circles. Then one day she asked me to go in with her, into the torture room, just to hold her hand, it would reassure her, give her courage while they strapped her down and put that plastic wedge into her mouth, so she wouldn't bite her lips or choke on her tongue. She gagged and thrashed, her back arching, wrists and ankles tugging at the leather straps that tied her down.

'But?' I dare...

'Nae bother', says the old anaesthetist upping the dose, 'it's for her ain good'. Then they put the pads onto her temples, the dial is turned and she jerks rigid, shaking and convulsing.

After that she fell into decline. Her black shiny hair went dull and started to come out in clumps. She had diarrhoea. Her cheeks hollowed. At visiting time, her family came to seek me out in my white coat, looking the part. But what part was I playing exactly? I hadn't a clue.

'D'you think she's alright?' they asked. 'She likes you. D'you think this ECT thing is working?'

'Oh of course,' I say. 'Matron will tell you ...'

The next week they wheeled her out on a trolley, a coarse white sheet covering her beautiful face. Bare feet sticking out. Going to her grave knowing she was a bad mother. A bad wife. A bad woman.

I mentioned before that there were geriatric cases in this psychiatric ward. A sort of overspill yard for old women stretched out on the rough sheets who rapidly developed bed sores because they never moved and their circulation got sluggish. The sores dug into their flesh, forming red craters on their heels. One day an old lady, agitated, waved at me from her bed. She wanted a bed pan urgently and there was no one else around so I heaved her up onto the metal bowl that I pushed under her bottom, and felt something snap in my groin. I had two blissful days off work in bed and then came back walking with a limp.

I came back again to this workhouse hospital, the following year in 1972 to collect my poor mum. She hated the place, knew the smell. She'd first come in 1967 when she'd had a large fibroid, the 'size of a grapefruit,' the doctor kept saying. They had to take it out and, to be thorough, they took out the womb and the ovaries as well, just to be sure it was all nice and clean.

But this time, in 1972 it was so much worse, this time my dear little mum had most of her guts taken out when they found she had bowel cancer. They created a stoma, an artificial anus, with a bag to catch the faecal matter, that always leaked. It was difficult to predict when it would bung up (when she took paracetamol?) or when it would overflow like the Victoria Falls (if she ate pineapple).

Years later, when her insides started to push out of the artificial anus into a massive hernia, the NHS gave her a straight-jacket corset that her arthritic hands could not pull on. My brother, the engineer, boiled the corset at high temperature and stretched it out over the back of a chair, but it was still impossible to get on. So, we brought her to France to see a gut specialist who said that usually with a hernia, he would be able to correct it with surgery, but in this case it was impossible, as they had pretty well cleaned out my poor mum's abdomen and there was nothing he could attach the surgical bands to.

I knew that place well. I knew the smell of it.

CHAPTER 5

1976: Don't Mention the Weather!

Bringing a new life into a country that no longer recognised itself was disturbing. And in 1976, England was disappearing into a heat haze. Look at mother-nature on the run in the 1970s. Ancient trees fell like match sticks and brown grass crackled under your feet. Over the Moss, plumes of smoke rose in the fields when the blades of a tractor struck a stone, creating a spark that set fire to the golden corn the farmers were harvesting. Just like their iron-age ancestors, they had discovered the language of fire.

Ken & Elaine - Paignton

Father, daughter and vanilla ice-cream at the seaside.

Adapting to a drought, an acute shortage of water, was traumatic for a country that was used to having too much rain. There were standpipes in the streets and quarrels over the appropriate use of water - washing the car, filling the paddling pool, sprinkling the bowling-greens-turned-brown? Cricket pitches that crunched underfoot, how would you know which way the ball would bounce? The first warning of what we would later call 'global warming'?

There were inconveniences undoubtedly, but many folks were determined to enjoy this unexpected warmth, toasting themselves in the sun, in the parks, on the beaches, wherever they could strip off. A Mediterranean tan was not to be sneezed at, and why block the sun with thick white cream when you wanted to go brown? The more precautious smeared on a bit of Amber Solar oil, to fry their skin better. A tan was so attractive - made you look healthier, slimmer, sexier. The price tag would only be revealed later when your wrinkled skin flowered with BCCs (Basil Cell Carcinomas) and the sun worshipers of yore took themselves to an ever-overstretched National Health Service. The weather was THE topic of conversation.

'Alright? Not too hot?'

'Gorgeous this sunshine!'

'Muggy at night.'

'We're staying at home for our holidays.'

'Who you sharing a bath with?'

'Phew what a scorcher!' Sub editors on the *Daily Mail* ran out of superlatives.

'Don't mention the weather', my mother kept saying. Her mantra.

On 5th August, Big Ben suffered internal damage due to heat exhaustion and the great clock stopped. For nine months. A complete gestation. An omen? Nothing good would come of this.

It was a tetchy time, with riots at the Nottinghill carnival, an uprising in Soweto and 'Cod Wars' with Iceland, as the Brits pinched the cod from under Icelandic noses. After thirteen years, the production of the iconic *Hillman Imp,* (my first car, remember) ended in 1976, when Hillman realised that it was perhaps not the cleverest of designs.

In many areas there was 'industrial unrest' and flies buzzed angry round the black rubbish bags piled high in the streets. Inflation rose with the temperature, recession was looming and the country heading for bankruptcy. The International Monetary Fund was called in for support.

'Don't mention the weather,' my mother kept saying.

On the plus side, the *entente* with France was still *cordiale* - we were building the world's first supersonic airliner Concorde, with our Gallic buddies. And ABBA provided the soundtrack to the sunshine. 'Serotonin in a song,' they said.

'OOOH you can dance! Yoooo can jive! Having the time of your life! sang the perfect Swedish blonde, Agnetha. So beautiful. Talented. It was depressing. 'The dancing queen, young and sweet, only 17!'

Legs swollen, breasts pendulous, I felt so old. Dancing in this heat? You must be joking. And then there was little Reggie Dwight with his podgy fingers, singing 'Don't go breaking my heart' with Kiki Dee in her dungarees. They were just perfect those two, but my heart was already breaking. Bernard was back in Marrakech and I was still waiting.

Waiting and watching these times that were a'changing.

1976 was also the year that Ormskirk's only famous son - apart from the Stanleys of course - Harold Wilson, former MP for Ormskirk and now Prime Minister of Great Britain and Northern Ireland, well he resigned, left office, gave up the plum job. Incomprehensible. Why would he do that? It wasn't even his party that pushed him out. The right-wing press clucked that there was a mega scandal about to come out (which was indeed true for Jeremy Thorpe, leader of the Liberal Party. But not for our Harold). No, Harold left of his own accord, perhaps because he felt the onset of Alzheimer's and knew his faculties were failing? Always a sensible man, he did the sensible thing and retired to the House of Lords where he chose to become Lord Wilson of Rievaulx (a Cistercian abbey in north Yorkshire, pillaged by Henry VIII and now a magnificent crumbling ruin). Pity. A missed opportunity that, when you think that Harold could have become Baron Wilson of Ormskirk.

Punk was born when the *Sex Pistols* found another use for safety pins (*une épingle à nourrice,* you remember). Mum and I sat together horrified, as we watched *Top of the Pops*, and discovered a lad called Johnny Rotten, who stuck safety pins in strange and painful places. People said that doing this gave them a feeling of freedom they had never imagined before. I just had to look away and walked out into the garden where the flowers were drooping in the heat.

'You have to stop watering now my lovely,' says my mother. 'You can't go on for ever.

'But they're dying.'

'All that bending and carrying isn't good for the baby, isn't good for you.'

'But grandad's pink hydrangea has turned purple and now it is going brown.'

'You have to let go. You can't go on in this heat.'

'I can't let it die.'

'You must stop now.'

I break down and cry and my mother tries to get her arms around her daughter, the size of a whale. At night in bed my legs stick together and the baby wriggles fretful. There is a pain in my back, a pain in my heart. Getting up for a pee again, the baby presses on my bladder.

1976 is not a good time to bring a child into the world perhaps. But then, is there ever a good time?

CHAPTER 6

Antenatal

In this hot, hot summer of '76, (five years after working in Ormskirk's former lunatic ward, remember) I now find myself, like a duck, waddling down Ruff Lane, past Victoria Regina's crotchless-underwear-park, with its monument to the heroes of the glorious Crimea and Boer wars. I push my bump along the busy Wigan Road with its petrol fumes and wait outside the old workhouse door, leaning in its shadow. An uneasy place. The morning sickness is long since passed, but I feel queasy and look for the AirFrance sick bag I keep handy. It's got shopping lists written all over it, but it could still serve its original purpose.

They say when you have a child nothing will ever be the same again. You become an adult. Ever vigilant, everything a threat. True enough, but in reality, it all starts at the moment of conception. When you are just a little bit pregnant you start to brood on everything that can go wrong.

Two o'clock on a scorching August afternoon they call all the expectant mothers of the Ormskirk and District area to the old workhouse, all the toby jugs waiting in line, stomachs on parade, hands supporting their backs. They have called everyone at the very same time. And woe betide you, if you are late. In these pre-computer days, it is too much to ask the hospital to work out individual, personalised appointments. The women might be late or not turn up at all and they-who-have-to-be-obeyed might be kept waiting. Expectant mothers and the great unwashed are always so unreliable. This is the only way, the NHS (remember, the best in the world) can function.

It is hot and the baby is curled up under my heart making my red face redder, and there is sweat running between my monumental breasts. The baby jiggles and my legs swell, veins standing out blue and black. Once you've clocked in, given your name, put your finger in the hole, you're trapped. You can't go back outside and wait in the shade. So, we all sit inside, in the heat, in rows, overflowing on narrow wooden chairs. Motherhood is sacrifice. You are the vessel, not the content. And the female birth equipment is a bodged job.

An hour and a half later they call my name. At least I think it's my name. You see I married a handsome Frenchman, a rarity in those times and they declare mine to be a funny name they can't pronounce and it would be safer just to call me Mrs Dee or perhaps Mrs Dubonnet? How about that then? Mrs Dubonnet? They all laugh. I agree. It's quicker that way … and anyway in a carefree past life I did have a penchant for the Queen's favourite tipple (made from heather honey and whisky). So those who could manage, called me Mrs Dubonnet, the others just called me Mrs Dee.

I have since learnt that this mispronunciation of my name is a form of implicit discrimination, signalling I am less important, less valued. It is a micro assault on my identity - too exotic, too alien, too French in Ormskirk. The experts say now that accepting anglicised versions of my name is associated with lower levels of self-esteem and can also be an indicator of lower levels of health and well-being. A clear message that I am not a normative member of this environment. But I don't protest. I don't correct them. Don't attract attention, it'll only make things worse. All I want is a healthy baby and a quiet life. (And to be honest, I have to own up to sometimes mispronouncing my own name, shortening Dubourdieu to Dubordieu. The experts tell you now that mispronouncing a name is a way of 'othering someone', which is probably true, but can you 'other' yourself I wonder?)

The nurse with the modern clip board goes through her list of questions.

'Age?'

'Twenty-five.'

She raises an eyebrow and twitches. 'Twenty-five?'

'Twenty-five.'

'That's rather old.'

'Is it?'

'Rather old for a primmy partum,' she sniffs.

I don't ask.

'Shoe size?'

Shoe size? Why does she want to know my shoe size?

'Four and a half,' I say. 'But at the moment I buy fives... I've got a very broad foot. And with the heat, and the baby ....my feet swell.'

'Make up your mind,' she says, 'is it a four and a half or is it a five?'

'Better say five. Be on the safe side.' But why does she want to know my shoe size? In case she has to lend me a pair of slippers when the workhouse door closes behind me? I don't ask.

Forty-five minutes later the nurse calls me into another

room where matron is waiting. I know she is matron because she wears that navy-blue uniform I remember. She has thick legs and her hands are folded over her solid girth. She must be wearing a corset to keep her stomach that round and smooth. Even in this heat. No wonder she looks angry. She tells me to strip off and lie on the bench. There is a man in a white coat standing by the wall. He does not introduce himself. I've seen him before somewhere, but Doctor Kildare he is not.

He prods and he pushes my baby, looks over to matron and says 'Breech.'

Matron frowns at her clip board and writes.

'Breach?' I ask

'Breech', repeats the man in the white coat.

Matron steps forward and prods my bulge, just below the rib cage. No 'by your leave', or anything like that. Just a hard shove

'Breech'.

'Breach?'

Matron's double chin wobbles above me. 'Baby-is-wrong-way-up', she mouths loudly, as to a retarded foreigner.

Wrong way? I knew it. Knew something was wrong. I'd always known, but couldn't ask the garrulous French doctor in Marrakech with a penchant for Chivas Regal. A disaster waiting to be born. The baby will be harmed. He won't be normal.

He wasn't going to be a thalidomide baby, because I hadn't taken any. But what I did know was that our garrulous French doctor had given me a tetanus jab before I knew I was pregnant. Would that mean the baby would be damaged? Would that mean he'd been harmed?

Matron prods again, hard and the baby recoils.

'See,' she says. 'Baby's head here, just here under ribs. Here.' She pokes. 'Giving you heart burn I shouldn't wonder.'

Giving me heart ache that's for sure.

'When his head should be here', she claps her hand onto my pubic mound 'Little scallywag.'

'That means', says the man in the white coat, 'that we will try and turn him. Persuade him to turn around. Right way up. Doesn't always work. Some resist right to the end.'

'Oh?'

'In that case ...'

'What?'

'In that case we'll give you a C section.'

'Medicine?'

'We'll open you up and pull him out the front door - though usually we'll try the irons first.'

'Like a slave ship?'

He reaches back and grabs a pair of big barbecue tweezers, with steel oval lobes that flash in the light. 'All mod cons', he says clapping them in front of my face. Snap snap. 'So, we insert the forceps ... up the birth canal'. He gives a thrust, like a boxer's uppercut and the irons flash evil in the sun. This isn't the Suez Canal we're talking about.

'Then we cup them around baby's head and pull him out like so'. His elbow shoots backwards.

'Unless baby shows signs of distress', says matron.

'Can...?'

'In which case we'll just whip him out,' says the man in the white coat. 'C section'.

'Sea?'

'Like Caesar. C section. Pull baby out the front door and then we stitch you up. Bob's your uncle. Or possibly it's Caesar's your uncle. Ha ha!'

'Can I ...?' I have to ask. I've been needing to know since we first found out, back in Marrakech months ago. Now is my chance to ask. To be reassured.

'Doctor is very busy,' says matron. 'You're not the only one.' She takes the irons from the consultant and drops them onto the steel tray with a clank.

'Can I? ... A question?'

'If you're quick,' says the man in the white coat.

'I had a tetanus injection before I knew I was pregnant. Will it harm the baby? Will it be damaged?' (Go on reassure me, tell me, tell me it's going to be alright, tell me I have nothing to worry about).

He doesn't even pause to draw breath. 'That is quite possible', says the man in the white coat. 'We cannot know. We cannot tell until baby is born. Until we pull him out kicking and screaming and get a good look at him. You see, anything that changes the meeloo (he said 'meeloo'. What is the 'meeloo'?) anything that changes the meeloo of the womb can have a negative impact on the foetus'.

It is five o'clock when I get out and the fumes are backing up the Wigan Road. I see a line of cars and they're all painted black. My baby may be damaged, will be damaged. But how? They'd never even thought of scans in those days. Or not in Ormskirk they hadn't. Two more months to wait. And the words stay locked in my heart strings. Anything that changes the meeloo. No eyes? Half a brain? Surprise! His fingers are missing. My Aunty Jenny had terrible morning sickness when she was expecting my cousin in the early '60s. 'You can try this,' said her doctor. 'Wonderful thing science. Can't hold back progress.' But she decided she could do without the pills and waited for the sickness to pass. Which it did. Good thing. My cousin Sylvia could've been one of the first Thalidomide babies to be dragged out, surprised to find that she had half a leg missing.

The philosopher Kant says you can measure the intelligence of an individual by the amount of incertitude (s)he is able to endure. Right. Not intelligent, me. Stressed out, flipped out by not knowing. Past the Disraeli Monument, Lord Beaconsfield, the favourite of the old queen. Author of *A Nation Divided* you know. But then again why would you be less intelligent if you can't stand not knowing? So, Eve wasn't intelligent? Big mistake getting thrown out of that lovely garden, that's for sure. But not intelligent? Not obedient, certainly. She just had to take a wee bite out of that apple/pomegranate. She had to know what it tasted like. So, if you can stand this not knowing then you are intelligent? Or perhaps it is, that you just don't care. I care. So much. But it's true I can do nothing about it now. The dice is cast, *les jeux sont faits*.

I walk back up Ruff Lane humming that tune. It's not so hot now. 'It is the evening of the day. I sit and watch the children play. Smiling faces I can see. But not for me.' And I think about Marianne Faithful and her beautiful, pure voice, and those kinky things she was said to have done with Mick Jagger and a *Mars Bar*.

CHAPTER 7

Finally...

I can't tell my mother about the baby. Can't tell her that her first grandchild is most likely damaged, incomplete somehow. To talk about it is to make it more real, make it come true, when there might still be half a chance.

The mornings are soft and dew shines on the silk maps the spiders weave on the fences. The summer has come to a close. The swallows have fattened their chicks on the glut of mayflies and are flying back to Africa. On the ninth day of September the blood red flag with the golden stars flies at half-mast. The father of the Chinese nation, Mao Zedong, has given up his ghost and moved on, while "800 million Chinamen cry" (says the newspaper). No one mentions the women. Were they allowed to have only one baby, even then? When did that start? And if you could only have one child then it was obvious it had to be a boy. This led to a lot of infanticides, getting rid of unwanted girls. Then there was a glut in boys and not enough girls to go round. And now this restriction has been lifted, the Chinese Communist Party today is horrified to discover that the increasingly gentrified working class doesn't want to have more children. Children are expensive to run and detract from their new life style.

Exasperated by the heat and the lack of rain, PM Jim Callaghan had appointed a Minister for the Drought to manage the stand pipes and persuade the usually reserved British to share a bath together. This was the right Honourable Lord Denis Howell PC, a man who had led a charmed life: a few years earlier an IRA bomb, destined for him and his family had blown up their Ford Cortina on the driveway of their home in Birmingham, but they escaped unharmed. So desperate was the Prime Minister that he even ordered the lucky Lord to do a rain dance, Morris-dancer-style, to persuade the rain gods to let down their water. This dance was a huge success, but a mixed blessing, as a few days later, the heavens opened and Denis-the-Rain-King became Denis-the-Minister-for-Floods as rain streamed over the earth, hard as iron and incapable of absorbing it. All this water sent the British in search of their wellies, cursing the government all the while. It was going to be a stormy autumn.

The seedpods that quietly swelled throughout the summer, are now bursting with new life. They crack and spurt over the hard ground. Perhaps new life should really come at the beginning of the year when it has a better chance of survival? In early spring the blue tits feed their young up to five hundred times a day from the caterpillars in the nearby oak trees, bursting into leaf. The male seahorse is heavily pregnant in spring, carrying his young inside him. When the full moon shines on the waters in May his contractions begin, so he gives his young the very best start in life, as they emerge with the bloom of plankton in the springtime. Not the autumn.

My baby will be born in October, a Libra, a law-giver, the holder of the scales. There were seventeen hours of daylight in Ormskirk on the 21st of June, but now we are into September, the days are growing short and the nights long. The children go back to school in their new uniforms, long socks curled around their ankles, ties asquiff. My mother too goes back to school, over the Moss and the polders to Formby, but at the end of the afternoon she comes back to me, stopping off on her way at the farm shop, or the market on Thursdays.

For medieval ladies, confinements started six weeks before the birth of their child and ended six weeks after the birth. Husbands were banned from the bed chamber till the mother had been churched. Easy enough in my case as my husband just isn't here. The mother-in-waiting had to concentrate on the baby that was coming, directing all her spirit towards him. They led the woman to her bedchamber, shut the shutters and barred the windows to keep out the light and then they took away the Arras and the tapestries and any other source of distraction, leaving the mother in waiting to wait. It is a funny feeling sharing your body with another being. You were used to having the whole place to yourself. But now you feel it wriggle and kick, hoping (s)he's fine in there or perhaps it's getting claustrophobic? It would be nice if we could just go to sleep, find a comfortable place and settle our two bodies into one.

I don't have my husband with me, but thank God I have some distraction from myself and the baby. I still have the telly and my mum who doesn't give me the medieval herbs (motherwort and shepherds purse) that the wise women handed out to mothers-to-be, but she does give me vanilla ice cream and raspberries, bowls of them. 'Good for your uterus', she says as we scoop them up in front of *Coronation Street*. Sit back and let the evening go.

And all that wonderful home cooking. No spam or packets or tins. No shocking pink Angel Delight or Bird's Dream Topping, but home boiled ham, and baby beetroot sliced into sugar and vinegar, roast potatoes and lamb chops in the oven, cauliflower cheese in creamy white sauce, Icelandic cod from Fleetwood and Ormskirk's potatoes cut into fat chips.

Occasionally she sends her best table cloths to the nuns' laundry in Liverpool. Was it a Magdalene laundry? A mother and baby unit? She wants to support their good works for those poor single mothers, and she is so pleased when our dirty linen comes back spotless, ironed and carefully folded in tissue paper. She is the best of cooks, the queen of puddings, rhubarb and apple crumble and custard, rice pudding and homemade strawberry jam.

Eating and reproducing - that's about the size of life, isn't it? With bouts of killing and genocide thrown in by belligerent males. But, still I cannot tell my mother of the disorder inside, not even on the autumn nights when we watch the telly together. *Morecambe and Wise* and the play 'what Ernie wrote'. When you laugh, your anxiety takes a walk outside. *Top of the Pops: Sergeant Pepper's Lonely Hearts' Club Band*, sit back and let the evening go. *Bohemian Rhapsody*, weird but thrilling.

When he is home, dad tries to control our telly viewing. He usually only watches the news, or *Z Cars* and then he gets up and turns off the TV (no remotes in those days.) No 'by your leave? 'Do you mind?' 'Have you had enough?' No, he just turns it off and walks out, even though we are still sitting there, obviously waiting for the next programme.

'Oh Dad!' I groan, prising myself out of the chair where I'd got comfortable for the evening. Perhaps we should have paid more attention to this behaviour. It might have been a warning. But I just turn the TV back on and we settle down for the *Black and White Minstrels* with their glitz and sequins, singing and dancing: all those white men blacked up for the show. Not a real black man amongst them, but we never noticed. It was just the way it was. And there is so much disorder in me, waiting. If you talk about it, tell your fear, it will make it come true.

We are all in transit. The baby too, but he doesn't know it. Do you know that infants babble in their mother's tongue? They can hear all of the 600 consonants and all of the 200 vowel sounds that make up the world's languages. Then they tune into the sounds that they hear most often and forget the others. Newborns cry with the accent of their mother that they heard in the womb.

Round belly, swinging breasts, I sing him nursery rhymes. The two of us wrapped up together. Quantum entanglement. Twinkle, Twinkle, Little Star. In bed the wind whispers lullabies. Ring a ring o'roses, a pocket full of posies, atishoo! atishoo! we all fall down with the black death when half the population perished. When the anxiety overflows it blocks my nose. I breathe through my mouth. But how can I eat? What if a bit of bread goes down the wrong way, takes the wrong turning? Then I won't be able to breathe. I'll turn red, then I'll turn blue and blow up like a balloon and my eyes will pop out of their sockets, or hang out on a sinew.

There is also liver and bacon from the butcher's shop down Burscough Street. Liver and onions and gravy and cabbage. You are what you eat. Calf's liver, the only one mum would buy from the young butcher whose wife Louise was pregnant with their first child. A boy hopefully, who would carry on from his father, grandfather and great-grandfather before. A grand life, an honest life, selling meat from the local farms, not drugged race horses from Ireland via Poland to make trafficked lasagna and poisoned Bolognese.

We all meet up at the antenatal classes on a Monday morning. With my lovely friend Jane we sit around waiting, giggling quietly and complaining about the classes. We don't understand any of it. And we're frightened not to be up to it. The labour. The birth. (There were no birth plans in those days. No 'Hey Google, tell me how a baby gets delivered'. None of that.) We've only got this woman in her white coat, the physiotherapist - at least that's what we think she is - telling us to pant like dogs. Why would we want to pant like dogs? We have no idea. It dries your throat, but it seems to keep her happy, while she writes out her shopping list on the inside of her hand.

She shows us a plastic pelvis and pushes a plastic doll through it and out the other side. Then she tells us to pant some more, tongues hanging out.

'Go on give it some welly,' she says, so we pant and then block our breathing when she tells us, 'because when you're in labour and the midwife yells push! then you push. Only don't do it now. We don't want to set off any early contractions now do we? Ha ha! And that's quite enough for one day.'

The class starts late and stops fifteen minutes early, but we're not complaining as we flounder about, trying to get upright again.

I walk past the Beaconsfield monument, through Victoria's park, back up Ruff Lane with dread in my heart.

Lie still

Hold still

Keep still,

oh

my fear.

It is getting cooler. In the early mornings, the ground is wet with dew and cabbages stand in the fields, row upon row, green in black soil. An impression of order. Beautiful regularity. Marching to the horizon, the great Ormskirk wall of cabbages. Calm, below a puffy sky, but there's always that smell of cabbages. In France it is a well-known fact that babies are born in cabbages - which saves the mother an awful lot of pain.

Lord Beaconsfield, Benjamin Disraeli wrote about love. Well he would, he wrote about most things. "What a mystery is love!" he sighed. "All the necessities and habits of our life sink before it. The lover is a spiritualized being, fit only to live upon ambrosia, and slumber in an imaginary paradise. The cares of the world do not touch him; its most stirring events are to him but the incidents of bygone annals."

Scary stuff, when you think this man was Prime Minister of Britain, Ireland and the British Empire and Victoria's treasured advisor. And before you start thinking that I am surprisingly well read, I should say that I can only quote Disraeli as my gran was awarded a 'Pocket Beaconsfield' as a school prize for regular attendance and hard work in 1907. My mum kept the little book on her shelves as it has a pretty cloth cover and embossed gilt spine. Now if he'd said "What a mystery is child birth!" He might have been nearer the mark.

Walking in the college rock garden, strange shadows hang from the trees in the low sunlight. Not where you expect them. And under your feet are the gilded leaves of the fallen dead. I'd read all of the natural childbirth books of course. And none of them ever mentioned shoe size.

'This is going to be OK,' said my husband, an adept of the Coué method. 'All will be well,' he repeated over and over, like a broken record.

'It'll be like pushing a letter through a letter box.' Though he has no more idea than I have. All I have to do is remember to pant. Like a dog. Do what I'm told. Yours not to reason why. Childbirth is a natural process, it is not an illness. Get on with it. The way women have done since the origin of the world. 'I am quick with child' the Bible says. That's a nice expression, but I am dead with fear.

Deadline for the birth. The date calculated by Ormskirk General Hospital is the 24th October. Which is nice. That's United Nations Day, Zambian Independence Day and my dad's birthday. Though it'll probably be later they say. First babies and primmy partums generally like to keep everyone waiting.

But the 17th of October 1976 is a full moon and Ormskirk's calculations don't take that into account. A damp October night with a full moon rising. I should have known. Quantum entanglement. I am cancer and a water sign. But when it comes, it comes with a whimper. That Sunday night when the moon is full, the bubble holding this swimmer in his quiet sea, well that bubble bursts. Did he puncture it with his knobbly elbows or a sharp right hook?

Maternity wards are full at the full moon when all the waters of the world are sucked towards that irresistible magnet. I've always loved the moon. It's the women's planet, providing the rhythm to our lives and cycles as the tides go in and out. But the moon is moving away from us. The moon is pulling away from us at the same rate as your finger nail grows: 3.8 centimeters a year. Perhaps that is why it is getting hotter.

There is a wet gush on the bathroom floor where a patch of white moonlight quivers. My waters. The ones I share with the baby in fact. Our waters break. Only it's not water, is it? It's amniotic fluid that bursts onto the bathroom floor as I'm getting into my pyjamas. So, I get dressed again. But there is nothing else. No contractions, not even the famous 'show', the bloody plug that blocks the entrance to your uterus and descends into your pants. None of that. Just the full moon and water and the pear tree holding its skeleton branches up to the sky.

You have been told that when your waters break you must go immediately to hospital as the once floating baby is now high and dry and vulnerable to infection, strangulation, suffocation and God knows what else.

This is the parting. The dividing into two, of that which has been one, for nine months. It is also the meeting. The rendezvous planned nine months ago. And what will this baby look like?

I go downstairs and open the door onto my mother's Sunday night viewing. *Up the Junction* or *Cathy Come Home?* after *Songs of Praise* and the news?

'I'm not sure,' I say, 'there are no contractions, just water. On the floor. I'm supposed to go now. To the hospital.'

My bag has been packed for weeks, ready by the door. As we step outside, it smells of autumn in the sharp October night. There is a shriek from the old pear tree behind the house. An owl looking for her prey - a mouse, a baby rabbit in the moonlight. The light is white. The moon close to the earth. Chestnuts plummet like sputniks onto the roof of the shack that served as a morgue in the Second World War. Long shadows fall over the car as we drive down St Helens' Road to the workhouse labour ward. You can hear the trembling of a star as it dies in the black vault above. My mum pushes open the door and that hospital smell smacks us in the face. Fear. Cabbage. Urine and disinfectant. What will happen? To the baby? To me? The die is cast. It was cast a long time ago in Marrakech but no one knows the answer. Not yet.

No, my mother cannot stay. 'Only the father may be admitted and he's in Marrakech, so you can come back tomorrow if you like,' they say closing the workhouse door in my mother's face. 'We've got work to do.'

'Right. Now. Let's get you cleaned up and sanitised. Spit. Spot. Strip off.'

You are at their mercy. You control nothing. Not your body. Not the birth of your baby. Bloody nada. Abandon hope all those who enter here.

'This is an enema.'

'Enemy?'

'Enema. A purge to clean out your gut. We don't want you defecating on baby's head now do we? That would be so shameful.'

'Hot shower. Really hot. Make sure you're clean. Don't want you contaminating baby, now do we? Or any of the other mothers in the ward for that matter.'

Hot shower and a shave. Pubic mound, large lips, anus all raked and shaved conscientiously. No soap or cream or anything like that. A few nicks and scrapes perhaps, but childbirth is not for the faint hearted.

Now what? Well, nothing. No contractions. Nothing, except the enema is still dribbling brown sewage down my legs.

'You'll see the consultant in the morning. There is nothing more we can do for you now.'

'I could have stayed at home in my own bed then?'

The bed squeals as it is pushed into the dark ward. Lights

out, curtains drawn round the beds, like a field hospital. The full moon shines through high windows throwing squares of white ice on the lino floor. Maternity wards are always full at the full moon. Babies whimper, mothers groan. There are memories in these walls, in these ceilings. The answer, my friend is blowing in the wind and there is a chill in the bed, cold with a rubber sheet under rough cotton. Figures drift back and forth, in and out throughout the night. This is it. Our time has come, but nothing is happening. There is nothing to do but watch and wait. Through the night of doubt and sorrow onward goes the pilgrim band. Singing songs of expectation, marching to the promised land. And I've still got you. Under my skin.

Six o clock next morning the neon lights flash. Babies scream. The tea trolley passes. Still nothing, no contractions.

'Don't be silly dear, you can't have breakfast. No. Not a cup of tea. That would be most unwise. We may have to give you a general anaesthetic. You may need a C section, we'll have to wait and see. In the meantime, you can live off your hump, can't you? Ha ha.'

Sometime later, around 10 o'clock the curtains are drawn back, the brakes kicked off and without a word I am wheeled back into the labour ward and hauled up onto the labour bench, long and hard.

'Feet in stirrups, open wide, let's have a look. Well, there's nothing going on down there,' says the nurse. 'What have you done with your contractions then? We've got to move things along haven't we or baby will get distressed. Not enough oxygen.

The big clock on the wall says 10.21.

At twelve o'clock the man in white appears. I know him now. He's the man who cut out my mother's uterus and ovaries and fallopian tubes and anything else he could lay his hands on. Said she had a fibroid the size of a grapefruit. So is this when he cuts the baby out? To see what he looks like? If he's got all his bits? His arms and his legs? Webbed feet? Hair lip?

'Oh no, not yet,' says white coat cheerily. 'We've got a few other tricks in our bag. Don't want to go cutting into the wall of the uterus unless we have to. Otherwise, all of your babies will have to be born that way.'

What other babies? The nurse comes back with a drip thing but she can't find the vein. 'Come on now, stiffen up,' she says, 'let's see your arm. Let's find that vein. Got to be here somewhere.'

Cold and thirsty, with a stomach like a bulging toothache. An abscess, throbbing. Are these the famous contractions then? That must be a good sign, mustn't it? But there's no one to tell me what to do. Should I pant or something? It hurts. My stomach goes stiff and I see the outline of a baby. And he doesn't want to come out. I'm so cold and this hurts and the baby doesn't want to come out. I watch the clock. But I've lost my specs. They told me to time the contractions, if that is what they are. Perhaps I should pant like a dog, but that makes me thirsty and they won't give me anything to drink. And the clock ticks on the wall.

At ten past three the doors swing open and my lovely mother appears wearing a gown and a milk maid's plastic hat.

'Ah ha!' she cries, 'success. At last. They let me in. I couldn't leave you on your own, now could I?' She goes and gets me a blanket.

'Your dad has gone to get Bernard from the airport. We rang the neighbour in Marrakech, in the flats. The one with the phone.'

Bernard has driven all night from Marrakech to Casablanca,

following the white ribbon of the road as it stretches out under the same moon. Driving slowly. Not his style at all, but this is no time to run into an unlit donkey-cart. He asks the neighbour to leave his sick note (prepared by the garrulous French doctor with a penchant for Chivas Regal) at the lycée in the morning. He puts on his only suit and tie. Look respectable and you're less likely to get stopped and questioned at the airport. If they find out he's leaving the country without authorisation in the middle of term, the Moroccan authorities will charge him with abandoning his post.

Dad collects him at Liverpool airport (not yet the John Lennon Airport - John is still alive at this point) and they have a scary drive back to Ormskirk. Dad is a man with a mission, but no spectacles to correct his myopia. He doesn't believe in them. It could also be that he's so vain, he probably thinks this song is about him. Thinks they age him. But the way he's driving it looks as if they're both going to die young and Bernard isn't going to meet his baby. 'Keep doing your eye exercises and you won't need those spectacles,' says dad. Like he told me to read Dick Reed's *'Natural Childbirth'* and all would be well. (Well, I did and it isn't.) Dad drives fast so he can read the signposts, then slams on the brakes before they whizz past. There are also the roundabouts that jump out at him at the very last minute. Bernard sits stiff in his seat. But the spirits of Ormskirk are watching over them and surprisingly they arrive in one piece at the hospital. Bernard jumps out of the car, shoulders his way through the swing doors, straight into the labour ward, smiling, reassuring. 'This will be like posting a letter,' he says, 'do not worry I am here.' But the doors flap open behind him and a nurse charges to head him off. My mother lets go of my hand and stands up.

'NO! BUT!' Yells the nurse, grabbing my smart suited, suntanned husband by the arm. Now Bernard is a judo black belt,

2nd Dan, and if ever he is manhandled, his reflexes are swift. His legendary leg sweep and strangulation hold have won him many a combat. I hold my breath. But she's lucky. Perhaps it is the steely glint of her buckle that does it, for he allows himself to be led away, smiling all the while.

My mother sits down and takes my hand. Then stands up again as the swing doors flap and my glamorous husband returns, suntan shown off by the white gown, though the milkmaid's plastic cap topping the curly black beard is a bit incongruous. My mother is told to leave. There is only one chair. Only one person can accompany the primipart. That's me. I know that now, and this is going to be a long business. They come with more gas and air (like Regina-Vagina) and the mask over my face puts paid to any conversation. And there is an injection. I don't know what. They never say. Is this the famous Pethidine? What is Pethidine? It's woozy and hot and my milkmaid husband with his black beard and suntan slips in and out of focus. I groan. And I call out. Who for? My mother? She's gone. My husband? I think it's him. He is here, but at a loss, a dead loss, talking about letters and post-boxes ... and the cock on the wall keeps ticking. Help to the helpless Lord, abide with me.

And the bairn? What about the baby? High and dry for such a long time. This has gone on too long. More than twenty-four hours. I scream, then fall back.

'Take deep breaths,' someone says. But here in the desert. The desert of Ormskirk I am so thirsty.

'Think about your fallopian tubes.'

'The size of grapefruit.'

Another pain in the arm. What is that?

Birth is a battlefield. In the desert of Ormskirk, where the sands and the cabbages swirl, birth is a battlefield. I feel it. Hear the cock ticking. Hear the baby ticking about to explode. His time is going to expire. I don't remember cursing anyone specifically but perhaps that could explain their attitude to me later. We're going nowhere. Somebody help us.

White coat appears floating, like ectoplasm. Floating and flapping. I am at his mercy. We are at his mercy. Is he going to cut out the baby? Pull him out through the front door?

The nurse straps my legs to the stirrups. 'Just in case you slip out of the saddle. Ha ha! Might close your legs and break baby's neck. We don't want that now do we …

Caesar?'

Caesar. Caesarea. A decree went out from Caesar Augustus that all the world should be taxed…

'No,' says ectoplasm from his echo chamber. 'We will save the womb. Save the womb for future births. You will thank us.'

What future?

'If we give you a caesarian now then we'll have to section you forever.'

Section me? Shut me up in a Victorian asylum? My husband won't allow it. But this conversation is beyond him.

They're going to give me ECT. That figures. They must give all mothers Electric Convulsive Therapy. No one in her right mind would do this twice.

Ectoplasm holds out his hand to the nurse.

'NOOO!' I yell and I twist and turn but I am attached to the stirrups.

'Irons,' commands ectoplasm.

And he thrusts in his irons. There is a tear - not a tear - a tear. There is a rip. R.I.P. There is a rip and a spout. Like a whale. Spouting. A red spout that hits the ceiling and falls back to earth covering the geyser in the white coat beneath.

'Oh do stop that,' yells the nurse. 'You're giving me a headache.'

Then plop plop it plops. Someone forgot to turn off the tap. Raindrops keep falling. So slowly. Rain drips, red plop, plop. Plop. Rain drops red on the milkmaids' caps below. Ectoplasm was right. He knew those milkmaids' caps would come in handy. 'You'll thank me later,' he yells with my blood dripping from his milkmaid's cap.

OOOH NOOO! I yell.

'Oh do be quiet,' says the nurse. 'Such a fuss!'

My husband peers at me with his black beard and his milkmaid's cap dripping with my blood. Beneath his tan, his skin is grey and he squeezes my hand.

The baby is stuck up the Suez Canal or is it the Panama? Walls fold around his head, trapped by the suction of flesh that creases and holds. Stuck. He doesn't want to come out. Who would? The white coat tugs, his thin lips tighten, while my lips are torn asunder. Maybe then I'll fade away and not have to face the facts. Return to the womb. To the origin.

The mother-to-be, the primmy partum rises, she rises up, up, like a barrage balloon over the Mersey, past that frontier into the unknown. She rises up to the workhouse ceiling, looks down on the scene below and sees two figures bending over legs that are sticking out at a strange angle. A man with a black beard is sitting at the bedhead, leaning in towards a face. A face, at first just ghostly.

The white coat draws back and regroups. *'Astride of a grave and a difficult birth. Down in the hole, lingeringly, the grave-digger puts on the forceps.'*[1] He repositions his irons, cocks a foot up against the bench and there is a roll of drums. 'Away, Haul Away!' sings Orme from his Viking boat on the Mersey, the border, the frontier to the underworld. And the white coat pulls and he pulls and he pulls the house down. There is a gloups like a fart. The canal gates open and the Red Sea parts. Holy Moses rolls down the mountainside carrying the tablets. Suction yields and the baby flops out. Like a seal onto the melting ice cap, landing at the feet of a polar bear. If no one has a pair of scissors then the waiting birds, attracted by the mother's groans will peck through the cord and eat it.

The origin of the world. Creation. The bairn flips out between the woman's bloody thighs, covered in white grease as if it has just swum the Channel. The whitecoat throws his irons aside, grabs the babe by the ankles and thumps it on its back. Appalled, the bairn shudders, takes a gulp of hot air that burns his lungs and he yells. His little face screws up and he yells and he yells. He yells for the both of them. For the pity of it. For the pain of it. For the disappointment of it. This is not how it was meant to be. Ripped from his mother.

A flash of scissors cuts the cord with a crunch and the white coat hands the outraged baby to the nurse. Then he lays his left hand flat on the mother's stomach, puts his right hand on top, flexes his elbows, leans hard on his hands and he starts to pump. He starts to pump the woman's soft mound of a stomach. Hard. Regularly. Pump. Pump.

The man with the black beard gets up. 'Surely?' He protests. 'Is this?' He protests. His wife lies lifeless. A cardiac massage in the wrong place? Is this? He attempts, raising his hand. But this is not his language. He does not speak Ormskirkian.

The white coat pays him no heed, but like a man possessed he keeps on pumping, pressing his full weight onto the woman's stomach exposed like a burial mound on the bench.

'Really? ... Is this?' The husband puts a restraining hand on the white coat as a large jellyfish flops out between the woman's thighs.

'Ah ha! There you are! See,' says the white coat, and with the practised hand of a fishmonger, he scoops up the jelly and tosses it into the bin.

(Nowadays there would be someone hovering outside to harvest this mana from heaven, take it off to a laboratory and lyophilise it for you. For a price of course. But then you can eat your placenta later, at your leisure, and savour all the precious vitamins and oligo-elements contained within.)

But here in Ormskirk in October 1976, it is the evening of the day. The clock says 11.20 pm as the white coat in his red milkmaid's cap holds up the baby for his father to admire. A triumph, a trophy for modern medicine. And through a veil darkly, his mother sees two pointed heads floating before her, and blood dripping from the sky.

'It is a boy,' says the specialist.

'Are they?' sobs the mother. 'Alright?'

'Well, he seems to have all his bits and pieces, doesn't he?' Says the white coat twirling him around. 'But we won't really know till tomorrow. See if everything's in working order. Never can tell.' And the two pixie heads disappear.

'Now, all we have to do is make mother comfortable. Tuck all these bits and pieces back inside and sew her up.'

Like grandma after she'd stuffed the turkey. Grandma would always sew up the cavity. Puck, puck and pull. Puck, puck and pull. A needle pushing through two bits of turkey flaps. Pulling them together. Stitched up with a darning needle and cat gut. The specialist applies himself to the task.

(Be assured Dear Reader, despite the name, no cat was hurt in this ancestral procedure. So-called 'cat gut' is a thread made from the dried intestines of certain unspecified, dead animals. But not cats. Cat gut was used to stitch up maimed combatants on both sides in the Boer War. It is said to be pliant and resistant when pulled through flesh, and capable of holding torn edges together till healing occurs - unless infection sets in and then the wound turns orange and black and fills up with puss. Cat gut is a bit on the thick side however, and can be an irritant. It does not dissolve, which means stitches must be removed later, manually).

The husband is blue and his lips are grey.

'You can be on your way now,' says the nurse. 'Let us deal with this.' She gestures to the carnage and the body of his wife stretched out on the bench. 'Go and tell the happy grandparents the good news.'

The husband is stripped of his gown and the dripping cap and is pushed out into the night. Nothing but the dead of night in this little town. Left to ponder all this in his heart. Alone. He is a father. His wife is mutilated. He has a son, but he looks strange, with a pixie head and a lump on top. This cannot be normal. This cannot be right. He passes though Victoria's Park and goes on up Ruff Lane.

---

[1]   Waiting for Godot: a Tragi-Comedy, Samuel Beckett, Paris, 1952.

CHAPTER 8

Some Memories Don't Wilt in the Vase

The mother is filled with opiates, poppies from Afghanistan, a land the British once held as a 'protectorate'. Funny status that. Not part of the British Empire, but that didn't stop them from protecting it. The trolley bed is pushed squealing, back into Ormskirk's maternity ward, where to all the porters and nurses and auxiliaries that pass by in the moonlight, the woman lying there looks comatose, dead even. Well I'll be damned, here comes your ghost again. One love. One life. But now we are two.

White as the sheet she lies on, rough cotton from the mills of Manchester or maybe Madras. Nothing moves, not an eyelash, nor a finger, not a twitch or a moan. She lies in the arms of morphine from the unquiet fields of Afghanistan where malnourished women hold babies with hollow eyes.

She hears it all, she feels it all, she sees it all. The weeping and the wailing. Mutilated bodies walk through workhouse walls. It is the evening of the day. She sits and watches the children in the concentration camps of Victoria's Empire. The Boer War. Tit for tat. Pitta patta blood drips red on the High Veld. Unversed in the subtleties of gentlemanly warfare, the Boers, make do and mend with what they have. They are Boers. They are farmers.

They have never been on the playing fields of Eton. They invent new tactics, new warfare against Victoria. Fly like a butterfly and sting like a bee. Sabotage what they can, then disappear into the night on their hardy ponies. Not good manners. Not real warfare. But what can you expect from boorish Boers? Horatio Herbert, first earl of Kitchener is nonplussed. He has to respond. He's been to Eton, he knows how to improvise. He sends his troops with their red coats and brass buttons, to the isolated homesteads to round up the women and the children, put them behind barbed wire fences and leave them there. On the veld. That'll teach them, their men folk, these Calvinists with long beards like the God of the Old Testament. Don't get me wrong, it's not malicious, there's no Doctor Mengele up there on the High Veld where the gold shines yellow in the African sun. They are not evil. They just forget to provide the women and children with food and water. The bare necessities. Compassion.

In the morning I come down from the High Veld, back to Ormskirk. What is missing? Something has changed. I pat my stomach. It's loose and it's baggy, my lodger has gone. But there's no cot beside my bed. There is no baby. I find spectacles on the bedside table and peer at the bed opposite. A baby sleeps in a goldfish crib beneath a white blanket. His mother lies inert, an arm thrown over her face.

They come to get me, two of them. Auxiliaries.

'No malingering. Can't have you lying around. Chop chop'. They pull back the bedding. 'Swing your legs around. That's a good girl. Soon have you on your feet. Come along. Now.' They wedge their hands into my armpits, crushing my breasts. The hospital gown leaves the bed with a ripping sound. The sheet beneath is red and brown. Burnt stubble on the African veld. The cotton sheet rises up with me, filled with the breath of life, then settles back onto the rubber sheet with a sigh.

'Where's the baby? What have you done with my baby? Does he have all his bits? Pixie heads?'

Sandwiched between them, the auxiliaries drag me past the lines of beds. Beds to the left of me, beds to the right of me, past crying babies and watching mothers. Brown lino, a sensible precaution for blood and body fluids. Streaked with black from trolley wheels.

'Where is my baby?'

'First things first,' they say. 'Nice bath and everything will look better. You can have some tea. A biscuit perhaps. Then nurse will bring baby.'

The gothic windows buckle and blur. Lines flow into waves and there is a splatter of slime, egg white on the floor. They wheel me around, drawing a semi-circle through the sick, dragging me back past the beds and the babies.

'You need to shape up,' they say.

They pull back the top sheet and rough cotton shines brown in the neon.

Some say the staff came from the workhouse. Others like my friend Jane, say they were Gestapo trained. But you can't say that nowadays, can you? Jane might, but I wouldn't dare. If you complain they'll make it worse. For you. For the baby. But where is the baby? Kindly, benevolent nurses, like the ones in *Call the Midwife* they are not. Why don't they bring my baby? What is wrong?

They come back later.

'We've run a bath for you. Five-star treatment, this. Get your pads and your pants. No messing this time.' And they march me to the bathroom. I see a face in the mirror. White shades of pale with purple underneath. They say I am a mother, but where is the baby?

'What you got in there?' Asks the auxiliary, poking my bag.

I tuck it under my arm. 'Stuff.'

'What stuff?'

'Toiletries'

'All that?'

'You know ...'

'Let's have a look.' She snatches the bag

'Oh makeup! Ha! ha! You don't need makeup in here dear! Who d'you think you are? Twiggy?' They cackle but I try not to listen. This is my moment for supplication. Let it be alright. Please just let the baby be all right.

Later a nurse comes carrying a bundle, wrapped like an Egyptian mummy. The shape of a gun shell. Pointed head with a lump on top.

There it is. The body that my body gave birth to. Small nose, puffy eyes with curling lashes. There is a flash of blue, like a robin's egg, then it is gone.

'All that pethidine,' says the nurse. 'Makes them sleepy. Enjoy it while you can. It'll soon wear off and you won't get any peace. Now we've got to get some colostrum into him. Breast is best. Sit up.'

But it's difficult to sit on cat's gut that has been thread through lumps of torn flesh. Down there. Somewhere. I have no idea where. No idea what is going on down there.

'We haven't got all day'. The nurse fumbles through the nighty to the nursing bra and like a rabbit from a hat, she pulls out one enormous white breast, criss-crossed with veins. Like blue cheese. The nurse passes me the bundle with the pointed head, all wrapped up in a muslin cloth like a bandage, going around and around the little body. But with all that gas and air and pethidine and whatever else, there's no way he's going to wake.

'Chop chop,' says the nurse stroking her finger along the baby's top lip. 'Let's get this show on the road.' She angles the baby's sleeping head, pressing its mouth hard onto the nipple with a stab of pain.

'Careful,' she says, prodding her finger into the inflated breast, hard like a melon, just below the baby's nose. 'We don't want to suffocate him now do we? Come on little'un. Open up.' She strokes his lip more vigorously.

The mother plucks ineffectual at the tightly packaged bundle. 'Perhaps it would be better if he could ...'

'What?'

'Breathe?'

'Don't be ridiculous, he's breathing.'

'Get his arms out.'

'Why?'

'His hands out.'

'Why?'

'So I can see them.'

'Why?'

'Count his fingers.'

'What for?'

'Has he got all his fingers?'

'Don't be silly.'

'He could hold my finger.'

'Far too young. He'll only scratch himself.'

The woman picks at the baby's strait-jacket. 'Is this? Necessary?'

'Obviously. We wouldn't do it otherwise, now would we? Makes baby feel secure in his swaddling clothes.' (So that's what it is, this white straight-jacket). 'If it was good enough for the baby Jesus, then it's good enough for the rest of us. And let's not forget that the Virgin Mary breastfed her child. Son of Man. Lamb of God.'

But she cannot rouse the sleeping bundle.

'Well you can put that away now,' says the nurse taking the sleeping baby from the mother. His pixie head lolls to one side as she lays him in the crib.

'Keep an eye on him at all times. Don't let him roll onto his back or he might choke.'

'Choke?'

'Choke.'

'What about the colostrum? For his defences? Protection?'

'You'll have to try again later, won't you? But not till after visiting time or we'll never get him settled.'

And she's off, leaving the mother to stow her bruised breast back into her nursing bra, roll off the cat gut and feel the tears run down her nose. Watching the baby all the while in case he chokes.

(Now I'm not saying all these nurses were uncaring. Perhaps the empathy had been squeezed out of them by the institution. Certainly they were not like Frances Brassfield who delivered a pair of twins under the mother's kitchen table during the Blitz. When a bomb fell at the back of the house and the explosion shattered the windows, Nurse Frances threw herself across the mother and the babies in the true style of Call the Midwife and Nonnatus House. But that was not the culture in the old workhouse in Ormskirk.)

Visiting time is from 6.30 pm, or whenever the bell rings after high tea, until 7.30 pm. No one is allowed into that long ward till all of the mothers and all of the babies are settled. Ten mothers with their babies down one wall. Ten mothers with their babies down the other. In the middle is a table with vases of flowers that get renewed whenever there is a death on the geriatric ward.

If one of the twenty babies is crying then everyone must wait till he is settled. Matron is strict. No sloppiness. Not on her watch.

Only one visitor at a time and there is a pecking order. Husbands first.

Loose limbed and tanned he comes, my beautiful black belted husband. He sits on my bed, holds my hand and looks questioning into my eyes.

'And just what do you think you are doing?' Barks matron rattling the rings on the curtain rail for better effect. 'Get off that bed at once young man. We'll have none of your continental ways here. Up! Up!' She pulls at the tweed jacket Bernard has borrowed from my dad. He gets up, puzzled while Matron tugs at the corners of the bedding, yanking it back into line.

'And I have to say that your mother is also waiting to come in, with some useful provisions, so perhaps it's better if you leave now young man.' Confused, my husband's foreign body is expelled. Then in comes my mother bearing clean nightwear, conference pears, magazines and Black Magic chocolates. When she reluctantly leaves, then my dad is allowed in for the last five minutes.

He looks aghast at his haggard daughter and the blue and red bruises up and down her arms (good thing he doesn't suspect the cat's handiwork on the under side).

'Oh!' he gasps, shocked. 'What have they done to you? What have they done? Where was Dick Reed?'

That actually, is a very good question. I'd like to know that myself. (Though I'm not sure that I want to discuss the ins and outs of my undercarriage with my dad.)

I've made a few tentative feels under the bed clothes, in the pants and under the damp smelly pad and found a bumpy terrain with crispy bits, like matches sticking out. The violence plays over and over in my mind. Thighs splayed. Flesh torn. That wasn't what I'd read. Natural childbirth. Dick Reed. Like when my mum had me in the back bedroom at my grandparents' house. Painless childbirth: the Lamaze Method. I'd read them all. But there were no real camera shots of real childbirth on the telly in those days. In the historical dramas or the westerns, they just told you to get some towels and boil some water - but they never said what for. Boil the baby? The mother? Make sure they were clean?

My dad looks at the baby in the crib and makes noises.

He hadn't been overjoyed when he got the news from Marrakech not long after we were married, announcing we were going to have a baby. And he was going to be a grandfather.

What about her career he asked? (I was sort of writing a master's dissertation at the time).

'What have they done to you?' He asks again, looking at the bruising along my arms.

How could I tell him when I didn't know myself?

(And don't run away with the idea that Dad was some sort of feminist. At parents' evening at Merchant Taylors' Girls' School with Mum, he went round all the teachers, including the needlework teacher.

'She's not very good at needlework,' says the teacher. 'She doesn't apply herself.'

'Well never mind,' says dad, 'as long as she can sew on her husband's buttons! Eh? Ha ha!'

'Harrumph, 'says the needlework teacher, 'he should be able to sew them on himself.')

'Benjamin we're calling him. Benjamin Ken ... after you.'

(But that was before we knew what he was up to, Dad, down in the smoke, away from the prying eyes of Ormskirk, with his floozy. If we'd known then what we found out later, there'd have been no Ken in the naming equation, believe me).

'That's nice,' he says. Matron rings the hand bell. 'Best be off,' he says.

My mother-in-law, Madame, that's what I always called her, Madame. Madame sends flowers to the hospital via Interflora. From Bordeaux to Ormskirk, but the language is not the same. She orders a bouquet of flowers in Bordeaux for delivery in Ormskirk where they send the flowers of the season, which are chrysanthemums.

A bunch of white and gold chrysanths with top heavy blooms. My husband is horrified. Can't take his eyes off them when he comes to the ward at visiting time. 'I'll take them with me,' he says, 'when I go.'

We don't get on, it's true, *ma belle-mère et moi*. Logical enough, no one would ever have been good enough for her son, and a foreigner to boot, but it took me a long time to work that one out.

This is the autumn, promising weeks of mist and mellow fruitfulness, and in France chrysanthemums are the flowers of the dead, used to decorate the tomb stones and remember the departed. The beginning of November holds the feasts of All Hallows and All Saints, when French families come together to remember those who have gone before. It is the most deadly weekend on the roads in France as families criss-cross the country in the wet and the drizzle to be together and put flowers on the graves of their ancestors. The chrysanthemum with its big brassy head would not be used for any other occasion. Only to decorate the tombs of the dead. For everything there is a season - a time and a flower for every purpose under heaven. And some memories don't wilt in the vase.

When the bell rings Bernard leaves. He takes the bunch of gold and white chrysanths out of the vase and looking thunderous, he walks down the ward dripping water behind him. Not even Matron dare ask what the hell he thinks he is doing.

'Must have been sent by one of her old lovers,' whispers a nurse. 'How very French.'

Bernard stuffs the funereal chrysanths, the national flower of Japan, into the bin in Victoria Park on his way back up Ruff Lane.

But soon he is gone. Returning to Marrakech and the Lycée Hassan II. The garrulous doctor with the penchant for Chivas Regal can't keep signing sick notes for ever. But it means Mum can come in every night. Dad's not in a hurry to come back. He's off to a meeting down in London. The rat. If only we'd known then what he was up to.

It is half past six and visiting time, but the visitors are still in the waiting room. Matron makes her entrance and points an accusing finger. All heads turn to look at Mum. 'It's your baby we're all waiting for,' she says. 'He won't settle. Again'. And no one is allowed in till all 20 babes are quiet in their cribs beside the workhouse bedsteads, their mothers sitting up straight, their hospital corners pulled to attention. 'It's your baby we're all waiting for.' Because little Benjamin cries a lot, now that the opiates have worn off.

(He probably has a twisted neck after all that time stuck in my birth canal high and dry, his little head getting more and more pointed, and the bump on his crown swelling as the inside of his head finds the only relief possible through the soft fontanelle on the top, pushing out through the only bit of cranium not welded together. Nowadays - well in France anyway - they would send him to a paediatric osteopath to straighten him out, realign his head and neck, put him out of his pain. But back in those days, they didn't have a clue. I didn't have a clue. No one had a clue in Ormskirk.)

The poor little thing he cries and he cries and can't latch onto my breasts that are hard and round like Charentais melons. Breast feeding. Giving the breast. The most natural thing in the world, a mother feeding her child. Well, *détrompez vous* (wise up, unmistake yourself). It may be natural, but it doesn't come easy. Though the chewed flesh and cracked nipples only come later when he finally gets used to clamping his jaws around the tender nipple.

And the nights. The dark autumn nights in the maternity ward with the baby alarms going off, one after another through the night. Like the shunting yard at Ormskirk station: shrill whistles, beds trundle past, nurses laugh, a mother cries in pain or despair, and the moon shines bright through high blank windows.

Last night as I lay on my pillow

Last night as I lay in my bed

Last night as I lay on my pillow

I dreamt that my baby was dead

Thor and Orme pursue the VIIth Earl, Stanley, his severed head leering, blood dripping from the ceiling.

During the day I have a table over my bed with a glass of water, a bag of conference pears, a box of Black Magic and some magazines: French maternity magazines promising painless childbirth and easy ways to regain your former self, your former figure, your previous life.

In the bed next to me, Valletta wishes me 'good luck' as we part company for the night. She was conceived as her parents sailed into the harbour in Malta and they wanted to preserve the memory of that wonderful night. Valletta. It's really pretty. *(Perhaps we should have called our son Marrakech? Maybe it would simplify things if we all called our babies after the place of conception. Humber Super Snipe, Hillman Imp ... perhaps not).*

The nurses descend, drawing the curtains around the beds, storing the tables at the side, 'so you can reach it dear, if you need it. Just here, inside the curtains.'

But in the darkness those curtains flap and rustle like tents in a field hospital, and disembodied hands appear through the gap, feeling their way, rustling Black Magic wrappers: Midnight Truffle, Dreamy Fudge, Orange Sensation, Raspberry Heaven, Coffee Crescent, and when the only only left is the elegant square of pure black magic, the hand hesitates, grumbling. 'I'd rather have Milk Tray'

Another hand fumbles for a magazine, 'shit!' it says, when it tips over the glass of water.

Some hands are discreet and take their booty back to the nurses' office. Others stand and giggle behind the curtain, flicking through the mags.

'Those Frenchies,' they say. 'Just look at that, quite disgusting. Don't even bother to shave all the pubes. How unhygienic is that?'

Most magazines reappear before the neon light returns at six. But the chocolates are gone forever and the babies whimper and the mothers groan. Discipline. That's what baby needs. Routine. A regular routine. Lights on at six. Early to bed, early to rise, and anyway the night staff have read all the mags and eaten all the chocs and they want to be home by seven thirty.

A few days after you've been shaved down there, spikes start to prickle. Where exactly you don't know, but bamboo spikes try to push their way through lumps of cat gut. A lunar landscape with moguls and boulders.

(In the Crimean War they put sugar onto wounds to absorb the infection … if they had any spare that is. If I'd known that, then I would have tried. Pyronidal cysts is what I'm suffering from … amongst other things).

When the pubic hair can't find its way out to the surface, it gets trapped under the skin and it festers. But I don't know that do I? All I can do is feel my way about down-under. Finding lumps prickly with crusty things hanging onto the cat gut.

I crack off some of the crust and like little Jack Horner, pull it out from under the bed clothes to have a look, surreptitiously, turning reddy brown flakes, one way and another. Turning them around in the light.

Dags. That's what they are: dags.

'Rattle yer dags Sheila', they say in the Australian outback. Look it up: 'Dags'. When sheep get the runs, diarrhoea, which they do all the time in the Australian outback, then brown liquid runs down the long fibres of wool on the sheep's backend, where the tail has been cut off and this brown liquid gets caked with dust. These woolly brown ringlets harden in the sun and when the sheep run, they rattle. Congealed poo in woolly streamers, that rattle like wind chimes.

'Rattle your dags Sheila' is a friendly Australian expression telling a woman to hurry up, get a move on.

That's what I've got - dags. Only when you lie, stuck to the stained sheet that never gets changed, they don't rattle. They just rip and crunch when you turn over.

Thank God for my mother's conference pears that keep my gut moving, getting the faeces past those stitches. The thought of constipation, straining against the cat gut, brings tears to my eyes. The nurse tells me that if the baby cries all the time, then it's my fault. He must have colic and I really should stop eating those conference pears. Chocolate would be so much better for baby.

Rattle yer dags Sheila.

An Interlude ...
Faeces, Poo and the Bristol List

(As for those runny faeces that create the dags, it was only twenty years later that a kindly homeopath in France raised this fundamental subject, so rarely discussed. Remember the Victorian handbooks on how to be a good wife, suggested the newly-wed spared her husband the unpleasant reminder of her bodily functions by recommending she only use the lavatory when her husband was out of the house?

It was my French homeopath let me in on a well-kept secret, worthy of the Free Masons. And now I'm passing it on to you: it is The Bristol List that draws up the seven different kinds of stools. (Not furniture but faeces.)

Why Bristol? I don't know (I always believed Bristol City was associated with boobs). The 'Bristol List' is strange, because usually when a scientist stumbles on an invention or a new bit of kit - then he claims it as his own and proudly gives it his name: the McPherson Strut, the Bunsen Burner, the de Dion Axel, the Petrie Dish...(I could press my point with the Guillotine, the Leotard, Pasteur-isation, the Phillips screw, the Sandwich, the Faraday cage, the Hammond organ, the Woodruff Key, the Ferris Wheel, the Bowler Hat, the Windsor knot or the Heimlich manoeuvre, but you might get bored.)

But here, strangely enough, in the taxonomy of human poo, the credit goes collectively to the City of Bristol. Pardon me for these ramblings, but you have to admit this is an intriguing byway which would make a good subject for a master's dissertation. This list must have been drawn up by a Victorian, for they were great taxonomists, liking order and tidiness in all things ... including poo. They were also great collectors of coprolites (dinosaur poo).

Apparently in the seven types of human stool established by this Bristol List, there is no pecking order: no stool shape, or form, or even consistency that is said to be better than any another - though as far as my French homeopath was concerned, the best stools (selles in French: various jeux de mot possible here, but we won't go there) the best stools were those moulées à la louche, shaped with a ladle ... like a good scoop of curds when you are making Camembert.

He also added that the best position to have a bowel movement (and that's another phrase that should attract our etymological attention, but we cannot stop) - the best position is not sitting upright, like we do on the modern porcelain throne, the best position is squatting, so the chiottes à la turque, the Turkish toilette - the hole in the ground with two pads to position your feet - the Turkish toilette gives by far the best position. The squat. The Turks were right ... if you can ignore the black flies that swarm out of the hole and buzz around your exposed posterior.

Toilets seem to be linked to national identity. In Iceland, appropriately at the Gullfoss Waterfall, there is this intriguing notice, which suggests the Chinese have other approaches to the question.

Always a sensible people, the Germans, have a little raised platform in the toilet to receive the falling poo. This stops splashing and also enables you to check the content of the poo that you have just evacuated - make sure there are no little thread worms wriggling about, or blood, or anything untoward.

Photo on the door of a toilet, Gullfoss (Golden) Waterfall, Iceland.

But whatever your position or your stool, there

can be no doubt that taking a dump must be classified as one of life's greatest pleasures. And you folks out there with an untrammelled bowel transit don't know how lucky you are.)

At night in Ormskirk's hospital, I climb the sands of the Kalahari trying to get to the high veld, but I keep slipping back and the baby must be somewhere under the sand that rolls over and over. The undertow pulls me back and I wake up panting. I can't breathe. Where is the baby? Has he choked? I can't breathe.

I press the buzzer to call the nurse. Panting, I wait for the sound of rubber soles squeaking on lino.

'I can't breathe. I'm choking.'

'I'll get the doctor,' she says and the rubber soles retreat at the same measured pace.

He comes, the dashing young houseman with his stethoscope dangling around his neck, and he sits on my bed. Good thing matron's gone home.

'Any trouble with your heart?' he asks

'My husband has gone back to Marrakech.'

He looks blank

'Total eclipse. ... Of the heart?'

'Oh. Right ... Apart from that?'

'A murmur. I have a heart murmur .... but my GP says everyone's got one of those and if I can run then there's nothing wrong with me.'

'And can you?'

'What?'

'Run?'

'Not now. But before. I could do everything. Before.'

'Probably all this fluid. It comes with the pregnancy you know. You fill up with fluid when you're pregnant. When you are up and about it settles on your ankles, but when you are lying in bed, it settles on your lungs. I'll tell the nurse to get you an extra pillow. That should fix it.'

(Perhaps. But since then I've had plenty others. Moments when I cannot breathe. In different places. In the tube. In Littlewoods. In the kitchen at home. Pricking sloes, watching the purple juice bubble out of the fruit. They call them panic attacks though I was really calm, just pricking the sloes. In France they call them anxiety attacks. I think that is nearer the mark.)

Once there was a way to get back homewards... Why can't I go home?

Why can't I push open the door, take my baby and escape like Nicolette with her beautiful translucid skin and bare feet ... Big feet! Look at the size of her feet. She wouldn't have trouble giving birth, and she pushes open the garden door to the starlit sky, and she escapes.

Edmond Dulac plate. 'Aucassin et Nicolette, 1903, Mais Nicolette une nuit s'enfuit'

Another bed is pushed into the ward that afternoon, along with a newly born babe in a fish tank crib. A young woman leaps out, her surgical gown flapping open at the back. Her hair is scraped back into two thick bunches on either side of her head. She pads up the ward, barefoot.

'What yer gotta do to get somepin to eat round here?' she yells.

We all watch from our beds, transfixed.

A nurse appears: 'Put your slippers on this minute, young woman.'

She goes back to her bag and pulls out a pair of flip flops and then she flip-flops up the ward yelling: 'I'm staaaaarvin'. Yer better give us somepin' to eat before I pass out.'

The nurse shunts her back to her bed and a quarter of an hour later an auxiliary brings a tray with a poached egg on toast.

'That all yer got?' says the young woman. 'I can see you've never had a babby.'

She eats the egg, pulls her clothes on, then with bag over one arm and baby in the other, she bangs out of the ward on her flip flops.

We all watch from our beds, stunned.

Stunned and jealous, as we lie there, waiting for the NHS to decide for us.

That night there is more shunting and in the morning, a new bed has appeared in the corner. On it lies a more elderly women, with a huge stomach pushing up the white counterpane. Looks as if she is going to give birth to twins. She lies quietly, nurses come and go and nothing happens. The next day they draw the curtains round her bed and we hear her groaning. Strange they do not take her to the labour ward. More groaning then nostrils twitch as a fetid stench passes through the ward. The curtains swish open and a nurse appears, carrying off the fruit of this poor woman's labour, a bedpan full of poo. The nurse returns with a long poll and opens all the top windows in the ward. The next day the woman has gone.

Mists rise from the cabbage fields of an autumn morning, rose hips red in tooth and nail, a shepherd's warning. While down Ruff Lane the pothole puddles are fringed with white, like doilies. But let's not get into potholes, they are no laughing matter when your undercarriage is strung up with cat gut.

It has been seven days now and I can't sleep with all these beds shunting, mothers moaning and babies yelling, and mine's not the only one who still hasn't got the hang of suckling. It's not the baby's fault my breasts are hard like melons ready to crack and he can't latch on. Poor little scrap. Poor little shrimp the French say: 'she's given birth to a shrimp,' (elle a accouché d'une crevette). It's not an insult, just a common French expression. People don't really think about it anymore. It's meant to be charming ... and it's true there is a certain resemblance with this scrappy pink bundle with a big head that bounces off my huge hard breasts.

Another interlude:
Breasts: an eternal preoccupation.

(Skinny and angular, the glamorous Twiggy ruined my adolescence. Flat-chested, skinny legs - she wore white tights to plump them out. The perfect coat-hanger for little Biba dresses and paisley patterns. No boobs, but so glamorous with that angular

haircut, high cheek bones and eyes the size of dinner plates. We all wanted to look like Twiggy. Though that was never going to happen, unless you bandaged your boobs flat the way the flappers did in the twenties, and the way the Japanese mothers did to their daughter's feet. But we could do the eye makeup with that fundamental lesson she taught us: if you want your blue eyes to look blue-er don't ever, ever, wear blue eyeshadow, it makes your eyes look grey and gives you tired blue circles under your eyes. If you want your eyes to look blue then load your lids with layers of green, preferably emerald. Then black eyeliner, heavy mascara and that arched socket line above. I got the little Biba suit, cream with purple piping and the white lace-up Viva Maria Boots. But I always had far too much bosom to look like Twiggy. I tucked it under my arms when I ran for the bus - a constant source of embarrassment.

In the sixties, T shirts with fruit on the front were all the rage - apples mostly, but I loved conference pears even then. One day, coming out of Littlewoods in Liverpool wearing a brown T shirt with a big yellow pear on the front, this young lad with acne, stares hard at my boobs and he says, 'That's a lovely pair you've got there love'. I blush red to the roots of my hair and swear never to wear that T shirt ever again.

It took me a long time to realise that boys actually quite like boobs. (Boobs are important to boys but then so are bums and if you keep quiet on the bus and stretch your ears back you may be lucky enough to hear them asking each other, 'which do you prefer? Bums or tits?').

But even for glamorous Twiggy, life wasn't all plain sailing. One night at a Gala charity dinner she was placed next to Princess Margaret - a true blooded snob, jealous of her own beauty. The Princess turns her back on our Twiggy throughout the dinner, ignoring her completely, till finally when the coffee is served, she turns around and she asks our fashion icon: 'And who might you be then?'

'My name is Lesley Ma'am', replies Twiggy ... 'but most people know me as "Twiggy" '.

'Oh,' says her Regal Serenity, 'how very unfortunate.' Then she turns her back on Twiggy again.

Twiggy was my icon, but she did me no good.)

It was only years later that I found out about Niki de Saint Phalle. I told you about Gustave Courbet, leader of the 19th century Realism Movement and his now famous 'Origin of the World'. Well, in the mid twentieth century, came the New Realists and Niki de Saint Phalle. Slender former model, then mother and self-taught artist-sculptor, Niki didn't hide her work under a frock coat like Gustave, but let her monumental Nanas frolic free in their femininity.

Exuberant and confident, Niki's Nana poses happily with Adam's serpent, that she had well under control.

She also created this picture of a pregnant mother and her baby, joyously snuggled up together. Liberating and life-affirming.

Only Nikki and her large, confident Nanas hadn't reached Ormskirk in the 1976. What we had were flat-chested, super skinny models. Some of you may even remember Vogue's oh-so-classy top model Jean Shrimpton, 'the shrimp', they called her.

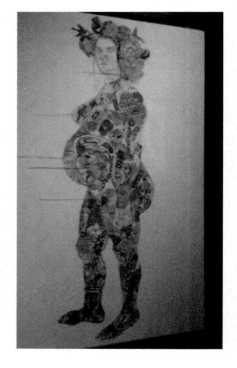

But back then in Ormskirk, it was my own little shrimp that worried me. He just couldn't latch on to my large breast, inflated so tight the nipple would shoot out of his mouth and squirt milk into his eye.

(For all of her nine children, Victoria-Regina-Imperatrix, had 'wet nurses'. Why do they call them that? The Queen paid women to leave their homes, come to the Palace and breast feed her off-spring … thus depriving the wet nurse's own child of its mother's milk. Victoria alway said she wasn't a cow - though in later years some of her nine children, especially Leopold, would come to dispute this.

But now I know that this situation could have been even worse. My baby could have been born, like Louis XIV, the Sun King (son of Louis XIII and Anne of Austria, who was in fact Spanish), with a front tooth already in place, ready to clamp onto any soft nipple that passed its way. They call it a 'milk tooth', but it's a tooth all the same, and it chewed its way through all the nipples that were offered to it. But as they were only wet nurses' nipples and not the Queen's, this was not a problem, and the court considered this early tooth a presage of the virility of the king to come. Which was just as well as his father, King Louis XIII, poor man, had been traumatised at the age of 14 when he married Anne of Austria, that Spanish Princess, also aged 14, in Bordeaux. The marriage had to be consummated straight after the ceremony with Spanish and French courtiers on hand in the bed chamber to assist the young couple with the mode d'emploi. After two hours this was deemed successful when a bloodied bed sheet (but whose blood was it?) was waved to the crowd waiting noisily outside the door. Poor Louis XIII didn't go near his wife for the next 4 years and thereafter he was said to dance down at the other end of the ballroom. Or perhaps he was just too flummoxed by the injunction to squeeze his left testicle at the moment of ejaculation, as scientists had informed him that the sperm that produced male heirs was located here. Either way, his son, the Sun King, Louis XIV (he with the sharp tooth) only came into the world 20 years later, when everyone had given up hoping for a royal heir and court gossip made so bold as to suggest that he had in fact been fathered by a man of the cloth, the right reverend Italian Cardinal, Mazarin.)

But for my baby, centuries later, being birthed is the end of the world as he has known it and he screws up his little pixie face with that bump on the top like a party hat and he screams. He can't latch on to my breast and sore and depressed I put him back into his crib, high and dry.

We call him Benjamin. That works fine in both languages. Bernard's father was a great fan of Benjamin Franklin, one of the founding fathers of American Independence, remembered for his work on drafting the American Constitution and his development of the lightning conductor. Always useful. There is even a Benjamin Franklin Road in Bordeaux.

Benjamin also means the little one, the last one, the baby of the family. And with my friend Jane and Louisa the butcher's wife, we all swear that never ever will we go through that again. (There's only Hilary in our group who thinks it was all jolly good fun.)

Though why should I complain? He has all his limbs, his eyes, his hands and those tiny, perfect nails. But how will he come to terms with such brutality at the start of his life? He howls and he rages day and night.

'You could always give him a bottle?' whispers a student nurse. 'Some doctors say that Formula makes baby more intelligent'. But the man in the white coat says NO. Breast is best ... especially in these parts.'

(Now that's intriguing. What is he referring to? The fact that a few years earlier, down the road at Windscale, they'd decided to dilute the cows' milk that was sold to the public, as a sensible precaution after a nuclear reactor in Windscale caught fire?)

'Worse still,' he says, 'you'll be going back to foreign parts, Marrakech, isn't it? Remember young woman, that mother passes on her defences to baby. It is your responsibility to build up his antibodies to fight those foreign bugs. What's more, the milk comes ready packaged, sterile, at the right temperature and just there, always to hand,' says the man, patting his chest.

The nurses keep coming back for another try, pulling and squeezing my breasts and pushing little Benjamin's head into my overflowing bosom. And yes, in the end, finally we get the hang of it … though little Benjamin always prefers the left breast, next to the heart and protests loudly when I unstick him and put him onto the other side. Always a leftie at heart my little Benjamin.

Now every time I stand up to rock my baby, I feel like my insides are falling out. Once upon a time I was falling in love, now I'm just falling apart. I press my hand hard against my Mount of Venus. Pain on the mount. I don't mention it and nobody asks why, when I stand up to rock my baby, I hold him in one arm, while the other hand clutches my pubis.

(Only many years later did I get an explanation of this strange phenomenon. These were the dark ages remember, no birth plans, no googling to tell you that In the middle of the pubic mound, the left and right pelvic bones are joined together, by cartilage I suppose, and this cartilage softens when birth approaches, allowing the canal gates to open and baby's head to pass through unscathed.

This useful bit of cartilage is called a 'symphysis' apparently. Nice and reassuring. Like a symphony, a sympathetic symphysis that shouldn't let your insides fall out. I also discovered later that it was possible after birth to pull your symphysis back into shape by drilling through the bone on either side of the pelvis, threading through strands of wire and then winching it all back into line. Thank God they hadn't heard of that in Ormskirk in 1976.)

CHAPTER 9

Mapping the Nether Region

*F*or a boy it is easy. Who doesn't know the story of Laurence of Arabia lost in the desert? All his men have died of thirst, and his camel Mustafa (as in Mustafa drink) asks him: 'All is dead Masser and you live. What you do?'

To which our imperial hero replies: 'Me no daft, me no silly, me drink water from my willy', which is also, as girls soon find out, a very handy gadget to have on a picnic. I don't know if penis envy exists, but willy envy, when you need a quick pee outdoors, certainly does.

The Cerne Abbas Giant in Dorset

The man and his willy, the male member, has always been out there, clearly identified, for all to see. Like the Cerne Abbas Giant in Dorset, put there by bawdy Benedictine monks. With his eleven-meter erect phallus supported by an impressive pair of balls, he towers over the surrounding countryside, pointing the way to nearby Cerne Abbey. This turned out to be a good bit of signposting because in the 11th century, Cerne was the 3rd richest abbey in England, as pilgrims flocked to the shrine of Eadwold of Cerne, renowned for his miracles. When he planted his staff into mother earth it sprang into life and sprouted, so Eadwold was the saint to see if you had issues with fertility ... and even today at night (if you see what I mean) courting couples will leap the fence and lie on top of his not so private parts to procreate.

For a long time, the giant with the enormous phallus was believed to be the demigod Hercules and a vestige of the Roman occupation of Britain. But once again, thanks to Open University academics (so thanks to PM Harold Wilson of Ormskirk) we now know the real story. The Cerne Abbas giant is owned by the National Trust who now let sheep do the donkey work, chomping on the giant's tufts, keeping a tidy bush, and making sure that his impressive manhood is always visible, showing the way to the abbey.

Some men are obsessed with their willy, even calling it their 'third leg', and like the giant, it is often size that is the real issue. If you visit the Phallological Museum in Reykjavik you'll see what I mean. Out of the 284 phalluses (plural? phalla?) exhibited, pride of place is given both to the elephant's and the aptly named, sperm whale's private parts.

Here, you will also find an elegant glass cabinet containing a rather large cod

Envious male gazing at the sperm whale's impressive member. The Phallological Museum, Reykjavik.

piece that the founder of the museum made for himself out of a sperm whale's penis skin. Clearly, he was proud, not to say obsessed, with his own member, which he later donated to the museum. The museum was anxious to point out that the founder did of course keep this codpiece for Sunday best, along with Christmas and ceremonial bow-ties, that the founder also made from the sperm whale's penis skin.

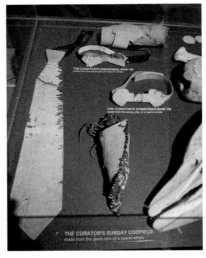

The Curator's Sunday codpiece, made from the penis skin of a sperm whale. The Phallological Museum, Reykjavik.

I have not found any vagina/vulva museums, nor handbags made out of labia, but that does not mean that men, like Gustave Courbet, were not interested in female, 'private' parts. Remember the sad case of the woman the Victorians called the 'Hottentot Venus', whose labia were put on display in a jar at the Musée de l'Homme *in Paris for many years. At the end of the twentieth century this poor 'Venus' finally regained her real name, Sara Baartman, and her remains were returned to her homeland, South Africa, for a decent burial.*

For females the situation is not as clear as for males: female genitalia are hidden away with a number of secret passages. In the beginning is number one, the first passage, out of which comes the wee-wee. Then there is the second passage, number two, which together with number one, is often collectively referred to as the wee. The two conduits being conflated. Then there comes passage number three, the bum hole, out of which come number twos, the poo. Are you following? So often, a girl's three secret passages are divided into two: the front bottom and the back bottom. This is strictly reserved for girls. Boys do not have a front bottom, they only have clearly signposted willy and balls. Generally speaking in the past, girls found it easier to refer to all of these subterranean tunnels, hidden by pubic hair and labia, as 'down-there'.

As the years pass, another whispered term arrives: the vagina. So you try to see if Disraeli (Lord Beaconsfield remember) mentions the vagina in his brilliant work, full of knowledge and wit. There was nothing I could find, though he does recommend that a man should talk to his wife to broaden his education: "As some men keep up their Greek by reading every day a chapter of the New Testament, so Coningsby kept up his knowledge of the world, by always, once at least in the four-and-twenty hours, having a delightful conversation with his wife." (I am sorry to say that I do not know who this exemplary Coningsby fellow was). Fanny on the other hand, is another name that appears regularly, so you thank the Lord you weren't christened Fanny and can now snigger knowingly at the play, Fanny by Gaslight. But it is only some time later, post-partum, that you become aware of the existence of 'fanny farts', glugging sounds from down under, which weren't there before when you did roll ups in the gym.

When you are young, you have no idea how all of this fits together and you don't dare ask the embarrassing questions. Why would you? Do you know how your heart works? It just does. Nobody ever volunteers the information. But in the real olden days long before Victoria, they knew a thing or two and even the saintly Augustin had worked out the female anatomy, proclaiming to the multitudes that 'we are all born between faeces and urine'. Which just about sums it up.

However, Merchant Taylors' School for Girls in Great Crosby in the 1960s had lost this direct approach to the female anatomy, and I don't believe the catholic convent school over the wall was any better. Although in the defence of '60s educationalists it should be said that we did do the reproductive system of the rabbit, with Miss Sharman in the Upper Fifth biology class.

But this is Merchant Taylors' School for Girls, the school that had thrown out it's only famous alumna (although technically speaking, are you still an alumna, if you were expelled?). Anyway, Beryl Bainbridge was asked to leave after writing rude rhymes in her rough book (isn't that what a rough book is for?). We never knew what it was she had written: a limerick about Willy or Fanny perhaps? Or 'the maths mistress is a dyke'? Perhaps not, they hadn't invented the term then. All we knew were the dykes that kept back the waters on the Moss road over to Formby. Or perhaps it was just 'knickers'? In an interview for Woman's Journal, April 1978, Beryl said "Once upon a time, when 'knickers' was a naughty word, and little girls were seen but not heard, I kept a secret notebook." Unfortunately, in July 2010, she moved on to uncensored pastures where she can now write as many rude rhymes as she likes ... and I will never know exactly what it was, she wrote in her rough book.

What we did learn about sex, we learnt from our peers, and those peers lucky enough to have mothers who talked about such things. Mine poor dear, came into my room one night when I was twelve, asleep in my bed. She put down a book, on the window ledge, on the other side of the room and said, 'There is something I want to talk to you about' - which actually was the very last thing she ever wanted to do, because the subject and that book were never mentioned again.

Then there were your unmentionables - which were precisely that: unmentionable. Menstruation - but we didn't call it that. Your monthlies, the curse - which is what it was, when you had to wear jam rags and a vaguely fishy smell would waft when you uncrossed your legs. Chronic embarrassment, that's what it was. When this brown smudge appeared in my knickers when I was thirteen, I told my mum who told my dad, who got the car out of the garage and took me down to Ormskirk bus station to catch the bus to school in Crosby. (Usually I walked, so this was different, I must've been a bit of an invalid). When I got out of the car at the bus station, Dad turned to me and said gruffly:

'You'll be alright as long as you are well protected'. And that was it.

Getting the curse was nothing to celebrate, no joys of turning into a woman or anything like that, but at least it got you off games if you didn't feel like running up and down the windy hockey pitch or plunging into the cold waters of Crosby Baths. Only later could you discard the lumpy 'sanitary towels' which were anything but sanitary, and replace them with tampons that your girl friends had told you about, as well as the technique of getting them inserted. This would only become easier once you'd had it, you'd lost it, you'd done it, you'd gone all the way and the path was thus opened up for a compacted wedge of dry cotton wool.

(Perhaps the one advantage of pregnancy is that you're relieved of the drudgery of heavy periods every four weeks or even worse in Zambia in 1969, high up on the plateau above the Zambezi, I had heavy bleeding every three weeks and I hadn't brought enough Lillets to last out the year. Something about the heat and the altitude, they said.)

Anyway, in 1964, in the lower fourth, one of the girls got pregnant.

'I don't know how this happened', Shona said. 'It's nothing to do with me. It's my boyfriend's fault. I got into the bath one night, after him, after he'd had a bath, and it must've happened then.'

A good life lesson we all thought. Don't get into the bath after your dirty boyfriend has been in. Get in first. But this was never discussed. How precisely had it happened? What had the boyfriend been up to in there, alone under the suds? And when Shona got into the bath later, after him, there must've been a vortex, a tsunami, a sort of reversed fanny fart that sucked boyfriend's sperm up into her egg? You never asked. You don't want to be laughed at. Not when you're in the lower fourth. Shona was expelled from Merchants' soon after, so we couldn't press her for details.

But these were heady days of discovery and meeting boys at Ormskirk bus station and finally being asked out on a proper date. Drinking Babycham in a champagne glass with a red glacé cherry. Babycham, the genuine champagne perry. Sounds like champagne, doesn't it? But it's more sham than Champagne. Not a grape in sight. Made from sugar beet ...from the fields of Ormskirk perhaps?

Even today people still hesitate as to what to call it: the Vulva, the Vagina ... both starting with a V you notice. Back to hieroglyphics, when the writing takes the shape of the object. Vagina is the most common. This comes from the latin vagina, meaning a sheath for a sword. The place where the sword is thrust. Which says a lot.

In latin vagina, logically enough, is a feminine noun. But curiously, when it turns up in France, that most Cartesian of countries, that most feminine of attributes becomes masculine: le vagin. And the most masculine of attributes, the penis, the sword in question, has become feminine: la verge ... Which then causes hilarity when busloads of French pupils going to meet nos amis les anglais for the first time spot signposts on the side of the road, warning them to 'Beware of Soft Verges!'

But it was only years later that we found out the monstrous impact of this lack of sex education on the lives of many mothers and babies.

Between 1949 and our fateful year of 1976, at least 185,000 babies were put up for adoption. These were the babies born to young unmarried mothers, 'fallen women'. The shamefulness of sex had to be covered up as the shame of a baby out of wedlock would be too much for a family to bear. So these young women were packed off to grim, unmarked 'mother and baby hostels' mostly run by the Catholic Church, far from their families. They were told they had sinned - the baby was living proof of that sin - so obviously they could only be treated harshly, punished even, made to do the laundry, the cleaning and the scrubbing of floors, right up to the day they gave birth. One young mother in labour, was told she deserved all the pain she was feeling. She had brought it all upon herself.

Their babies were taken from them at 10 weeks, and put up for adoption, some to good families, some not. Some were sent far away … Australia, Canada, New Zealand. These children were told their mothers didn't want them and the children carried this sadness with them all their lives.

The whole operation was shrouded in shame and secrecy - often names were changed so the adoption papers did not correspond to the birth certificates, thus depriving these children of their identities and making it difficult for them to find their birth mothers in later life. There were also other practical considerations, like when they were asked about their family's medical history, they were unable to give it.

These young mothers then returned home, alone. They were told to act as if nothing had happened, but they carried their trauma and loss with them for the rest of their lives. One mother later asked, why she hadn't had any other children, replied: 'Because I only wanted him. He was the only one I wanted.'

And where was the father in all of this, you may ask? Well, he was just a bit of a lad, wasn't he? It was just the way it was back then, when there was precious little contraception and no sex education. Women had no information and no choice.

Nowadays we have Gogglebox - that is the new sex education for people like me. If you watch it on a day when they're showing clips from Naked Attraction you'll get to see all those down-theres, all shaved and waxed, in magnified close up - sometimes even with bells and rings and studs pierced through them. Painful mutilation. Why would anyone want to do that?

Gustave Courbet, who liked a luxuriant bush remember, would not have approved. But it might have reassured John Ruskin, who was enthralled by Botticelli's classical painting, The Birth of Venus, as the goddess of beauty and desire, emerges from the waves, her hair cascading down over her totally bald mount of Venus. Ruskin took fright on his wedding night when he discovered that his wife Effy had a different configuration down-there, and a threatening thatch of pubic hair.

This creation of Venus as a fully formed woman without any pubic hair, was the archetype of feminine beauty at the Renaissance, and if you watch Naked Attraction, you will realise that it remains so today.

When did this happen exactly, the stripping of the pubes? A full Brazilian? When did it come into vogue, when contenders on Naked Attraction would gasp in horror if presented with an authentic bushy bush? It is hard to know because back in my day, girls didn't go around flashing their down-theres. Yet nowadays they've all got to get rid of every strand of body hair. If you shave it, it grows back prickly - so you've got to wax it off, which is bloody painful. Whichever beautician persuaded girls to do this was a genius, generating huge amounts of income. And now finally, what makes me laugh - and I know I shouldn't - but the thing is, what makes me laugh, is that men too have recently been conned into this shaving and waxing malarky as well - all hairless like the Chippendales. So, what's wrong with a bit of chest hair? You don't necessarily have to have the gold medallion nesting in there as well, like Magnum, who always left his shirt open to reveal his riot of fluff. True alpha male. The way God intended. It must also be the same beautician who persuaded all the young girls to have a full Brazilian, who has now persuaded them to pluck out their eyebrows and replace them with huge pencilled arcs and false eyelashes, like the dame at the panto. Clever. Beauticians. They know how to drum up trade.

Today with Gogglebox we are blessed with Jenny and Lee, the Malone family and Sophie and her little brother Pete, sitting on their sofas, commenting on what they see on the telly. They are the new pedagogues, the vectors of otherwise unsuspected (well, to me at least) new trends and neologisms. They are not entomologists, studying bugs, but the new etymologists, studying words.

It was Jenny, who from the sofa of her friend Lee's mobile home in Hull, pronounced for the first time in my hearing, the word: 'lady piece'. That's nice. So that's what half of humanity has got down-there? A lady piece. Not a smelly old cod piece, but a nice 'lady piece'. It's amazing what you can learn from television: How to re-couple on Love Island. How to build a Sex Room in your house. How nowadays, all mothers in labour seem to be given an epidural. They stick a needle into your spinal cord and dis-activate the lower part of your body.

They seem to have got the hang of it now. Before there was a danger you might end up paralysed. You don't feel a thing. And strangely enough, they also put up a tent, a huge blue screen around the mother at waist height. You can't feel anything - we've established that - but you can't see anything either. The mother is totally disconnected from this hi-tech birthing process, while the medics are left to get on down there, in her nether region. So, it's all a big surprise when they yank the baby out and everything goes quiet. The mother starts panicking because there's no noise: they've stopped talking and the baby isn't screaming. Why isn't the baby screaming? Then they go 'Surprise! Look what we found'. And the baby screams and appears from behind the blue tent, like a rabbit out of a hat.

CHAPTER 10

Going Home

My mum comes every night after work with conference pears, a clean nursing bra, thick pads and knickers and nighties which get soiled immediately on the dirty cotton that covers the rubber sheeting beneath. The workhouse mattress must be protected at all costs. Like most mothers back then, I stayed in that hospital for ten days and not once did they change those bloody sheets.

At night the traffic on the Wigan Road stops and the rhythm of darkness reclaims its rights. What was it exactly that Gerontius dreamt of? A sensible scientist putting filters onto those piles up the road at Windscale? Without those filters we'd have been the world's first major nuclear accident, long before Chernobyl. Only we didn't know that then. Perhaps white coat with his 'breast is best', perhaps he had some idea?

If you leave Ormskirk on the Wigan Road, going towards the lakes carved out of the land by the great glaciers, you may hear tell that on the 10th of October 1957, a huge fire broke out at the two-pile Windscale 'Facility'. Facilitating what you may ask? Facilitating the making of Einstein's atomic bomb. Quantum entanglement with the Americans of course. But one engineer had a premonition, a dream and he capped those piles with filters, though nobody told him to do so. But despite this the fire raged on for three days, releasing radioactive particles, carried by the westerlies over Britain and Europe. Only nobody mentioned it. The Prime Minister, 'you've-never-had-it-so-good-Harold-Macmillan', didn't want to jeopardise his relations with Uncle Sam. But the radioactive isotope iodine 131, which "may lead" to cancer of the thyroid - let's not overreact here - did concern a few people. No one was evacuated from the surrounding area but as a precaution, the milk from the cows on the 500 square kilometres (190 square miles) of pastures surrounding the plant was diluted. Some farmers even went so far as to tip all of their milk production down the drain for one whole month. But the government kept stum ... just as they had done for all the other radioactive 'incidents' in the years preceding this fire.

Windscale in Cumberland finally got a make-over and became Sellafield in Cumbria, but plankton still glows green in the Irish Sea. While closer to home in Ormskirk, locals were more preoccupied by the bundles of raw sewage that swung in with the tide up the Mersey estuary. There were no dignified Gormley statues then on Crosby beach, just triangular spikes of concrete to stop enemy aircraft from landing. And a sign telling you to Beware of the Quick Sands! The quick and the dead that Orme never noticed when he waded ashore.

Another dismembered hand feels its way through the curtain and taps along the bedside table. Feeling. Rustling a chocolate out of the box. Compulsive behind the curtain. It has flicked through the magazines and it doesn't like conference pears, but it always knows when a new box of Black Magic has appeared.

In the morning, fingers of light penetrate, scratching the walls, the last fling of red and pink. And just when I'd given up, given up asking, asking when I could go home and had resigned myself to this no man's land, the man himself, the man in the white coat appears and he asks: 'What's that?'

'A book.'

'Oh?'

'Pat Barker.'

'What's that about then?'

'There's this woman... A woman who can't express herself.'

'Should get a breast pump then, shouldn't she? Ha ha!' (Pause.) 'Well I suppose we can let you go now,' he says. 'Get your GP to take out those stitches.'

'When?'

'Later.'

'When later?'

'When they are ready'.

That's it. They are letting us out. Out of the neon light and the shunting yard of creaking beds and moaning. The autumn wind blows chilly and cold. Shaken and trampled, but we have survived. I just had too many expectations. Wrong expectations. No one tells you birth is a battlefield.

The baby squints, wrapped in the white blanket my Granny has crochéd. Low in the sky a white disc glows behind the trees. A space ship lands. There is a strange stillness and the baby is quiet as we step into the light. Once there was a way to get back homewards. Once there was a way to get back home, sweet pretty darling do not cry, and I will sing a lullaby.

Who came to collect us? I can't be sure, but it must've been my mum who came to take us home. Dad would have been in a meeting. She hated driving. Got her licence at 40, at the third attempt, because she had to be able to drive to work in Formby, across the Moss, the farm land reclaimed from the sea, with its polders and dykes, where one dark night the heir to the Littlewoods' fortune was driving his flashy sports car, with Miss Liverpool snug at his side. They were taking the short cut, from Aughton to Southport across the Moss, but he missed one of the hairpin bends and the car shot off the road and sank in a ditch. He scrambled free but Miss Liverpool was trapped in the car and drowned in the muddy waters. My mum kept reminding me of that.

Now a robin sings. The robins from northern Europe have arrived for the winter so it is important that local birds defend their territory. What is exceptional with robins is that even the females sing. I've got my baby and my mum has come to take us home. Not like the poor folks around the corner in the psychiatric ward, locked up and convulsed. They'll let them out perhaps when they need a bed. Sputnik conkers drop through the leaves, sinking their spikes into the earth. It's hard to walk with catgut pulling at your down-there. Geese fly overhead in a jagged V formation, chatting on their way back south.

We made it. Survived the workhouse. Together. We are out. We pass through Ormskirk. Sense the history beneath us. The peoples, the settlements, the ruins - nothing is permanent. Nothing lasts forever. But Ormskirk salutes this new generation as it passes by.

CHAPTER 11

Splicing Cat Gut

He's got all of his bits and pieces in working order they say, but he won't stop crying. Why won't he stop crying? Colic they say. He cries, pulling his little knees up to his chest. It's his mother's fault, eating all the wrong things, especially those conference pears that go straight into her milk, like Isotope Iodine 131. But I can't manage without them. Not emotionally charged like the apple, the pear is the best way to get a nice soft crap. Only this issue was never raised in the hospital, except perhaps by White Coat who enigmatically enquired one day if I had passed a motion. 'Not recently,' I say, 'the last one was probably at the school debating society.' He gives a faint smile and moves on.

My Mum is there and she does all the cooking, just there are no more onions or garlic or cabbage or sprouts or cauliflower. But still he cries, and at night my Mum goes to bed and she shuts the door. She needs her sleep because next day she drives across the Moss to do a full day's work at school.

Breast is best for the baby, there is no doubt about that, with the milk bar, the milk cow on tap all the time. And that's another thing they don't tell you. When you decide to breastfeed, you've made yourself irreplaceable. Your husband can't do it. He's in Marrakech and anyway all that black chest hair would tickle the baby. No one else can do it, not even if you squeeze out some milk ('express it', is the term) for someone else to give him so you can get some sleep. Not that there is anyone to take over at night, but even in the daytime it doesn't work. Benjamin never took to plastic and would push the teat out of his mouth with his tongue. Only flesh would do for this babe, right up until he started sprouting teeth. He was weaned at nine months. Went straight from the breast to the spoon - no plastic teats for him.

There were no parenting classes in those days (unless you count the half hour we spent watching the physio slosh water over a plastic doll in a bathtub). There was only Mum and the legendary Doctor Benjamin Spock ... who was no help at all. Dr Spock (and that was a funny name, even before *Star Wars*) was the paediatric guru who had written his *Baby and Childcare handbook*, declared to be the 'greatest best seller since best seller lists began'. In 1975 he had sold over 20 million copies to desperate parents. But he just made you feel you were doing it all wrong. Like he said baby should always be bathed before 10 o'clock in the morning. What sort of a plan was that? He said it was better for baby, and for you, as you don't want to go stimulating baby just before bedtime. But your intuition tells you to bath him at night, just before bedtime. Only now Dr Spock makes you feel guilty...

My down-there is trashed and I don't think I'll ever walk normal again. As for sex it doesn't bear thinking about. That's what got me into this mess in the first place. Nor take a satisfying dump: a peaceful number two is a thing of the past. They just pulled the baby out of the garage and the roof fell in. He cries all the time. As I said before, he was probably suffering from damage to his neck and post-traumatic stress, only they hadn't invented it back then. A good day is when I can get up, wash my hair and go back to bed, taking the baby with me. Survival is salvaged from little victories. One day at a time, sweet Jesus.

When he cries my breasts answer his call, tingling and dribbling. As I get up the dags between my legs pull away from the pad like a plaster. Ripping. And it will be the same, tomorrow and the night after that and the day after that. Dealing with the pain. Counting out the days and nights in *Solpadeines* that my mum gives me. In a glass of water the holy pastel sinks to the bottom, then sends up desperate lines of bubbles. Semaphore signals. The pastel starts to tremble, fizzing and frothing, till like a communion wafer, it rises to the surface and shivers expectant. Wait. Not yet. Delay the rush, the release when the bubbles latch onto the pain and break it apart. My mum got hooked on these opiates after she'd had her gut taken out in Ormskirk General hospital in 1972. Now it's my turn.

It is the evening of the day

I sit and hear the baby cry

Silent faces float around

Tears falling on the ground

I sit and watch as tears go by.

Sleep deprivation is the first weapon of the sadist and the torturer. I never get more than two hours sleep, day or night. I am not Napoleon. I am not Margaret Thatcher. I need more than 2 hours sleep a night. I take him into bed with me, just for a little while. Like shutting your eyes when you're driving, it's just for a little while. And if by chance he falls asleep at the breast then I can shut my eyes too.

Feeding your own child, giving him your breast - not somebody else's, not a wet nurse's, not a bottle, giving him your breast every 2 hours day and night.

I push back the last feed to 12 pm and hope he'll sleep

through till 4 of even 5 am. That would be great, but it doesn't happen. He cries again at 2 am and then at 4 am when you change the nappy, put the green poo down the loo and the terry towelling nappy into the bucket to soak, then change his wet sheet with one hand while holding in your symphysis with the other.

'Well that's quite normal', says the health visitor when she finally comes to visit. 'Two hours is a whole sleep cycle. Quite natural. Enjoy your baby, that's what you must do. Enjoy this time together. Soon he'll be grown-up and gone. Before you can turn around. He'll be grown up and gone.'

Well from where I'm standing it doesn't feel like that: feeds every 2 hours with a baby that falls asleep at the breast, but when I put him back down in his cot he yells and he screams and he thrashes about. The only thing that seems to calm him is movement. Walking around, holding my symphysis in place. When I do get to bed I wake up patting the covers beside me, looking for the baby, trying to find the baby. I must have smothered the baby, rolled on top of him, smothered the baby. He's somewhere in the bed clothes. Strangely I find him in his cot. He's not crying and he's not moving so I snatch him out and clutch him to me. Is he breathing? Dear God is he breathing? Yes he's breathing, and now he's crying. First rule never wake a sleeping babe unless you think he's dead.

Kneeling in front of the baby trying to change the towelling nappy, tears dropping onto his round tummy and bulging umbilical cord clamped with some sort of metal clip. The baby is howling and his nappy is full of green slime. When I'm done, I dump the inconsolable babe back in his cot, and flop onto my bed, hands over my ears, staring at the ceiling.

And when you put him down in his cot, remember, don't ever

lie him on his back. If he sicks up your breast milk, which inevitably he will, then he'll choke. Lie him on his side or on his stomach (though later the experts declared that this was responsible for many cot deaths, as the baby couldn't breathe). Never-ever lie him on his back. But sometimes you find him, and he's rolled over onto his back all by himself. How is it possible for such a tiny scrap to survive?

Nothing can prepare you for this. No one tells you. You wouldn't believe them if they did. A bomb explodes. Your whole life has gone overboard, and your body is wrecked. I said before, the world is divided into two groups. Those who have given birth and those who haven't. Your world has changed forever and there is no going back.

My lovely little granny lives on the other side of the garden wall: all four feet eleven of her when she stands on the tiptoes of her tiny feet. Size two and a half. (The family doctor had to use 'the irons' when she gave birth to my mum). She always wore stilettos.

The Principal's House at Edge Hill College was built for dad, the first male principal of the college and the first to come with a family. It was an architect's house and when my granny came round she tapped out her semaphore on the first real parquet flooring we'd ever seen. The architect was horrified:

'Tell your mother', he said to my mum (he was frightened of dad), 'tell your mother to put on her slippers when she enters this house: it looks like a mad woodpecker's been at my beautiful parquet flooring.'

Apart from that one joke, he wasn't a bundle of laughs and had not been amused when my parents would come out under cover of darkness from Dr Bane's flat (the former principal's flat was our temporary accommodation in the college) to move the marker pegs for the foundations of the new house to another spot that they preferred. It turned out later that we were the only family ever to live in that house. After dad cleared off to the smoke, pursuing his lost youth, the next principal, wise man, did not want to live on campus and the house became a teaching centre before being pulled down to make room for a larger development.

Back in my carefree days I was always running in and out of my granny's bungalow next door. But now that I couldn't stand up for long, I didn't get to see her very often as she had trouble getting up the stairs. Bad hips. All those stilettos had put them out of joint. But one afternoon she comes over to see if she can help. I'm in bed dozing and the baby, miraculously is sleeping.

'Hello pet,' says she. 'I thought I'd just pop over to see if there's anything I can do. Change the baby's nappy, shall I?

'Well he's asleep at the moment.'

'Then you won't have to do it when he wakes up will you? Every little bit helps,' and she scoops him up and plonks him on the bed beside me.

'One thing less for you to do.'

The baby's head wobbles and he squints at her as she opens up the *babygrow*.

'Amazing these things,' she says. 'Never had them in my day. Keeps his little back nice and warm.' She undoes the safety pin and takes off the terry towelling nappy.

'You just hold him there steady,' she says, 'while I go and get some warm water to wash him.' Benjamin sits there, head lolling, surprised.

She returns with the bowl of water and lays him on his back and washes his little willy which stands up on parade and squirts all over her hands and my sheet.

'Oh, you little rascal,' she giggles slopping the bowl of water onto his stomach. The baby gives a sort of lopsided smile and lets off a squirt of brown liquid over the duvet, spattering my nighty.

Granny looks at it, perplexed. 'You should watch what you're doing pet. You can't go eating them pears. It's giving him the runs.' She looks around. 'Ooh is that the time? Got to get your granddad his tea. Old folks are like babies, you know petal. You've got to establish a routine.' She rummages in her pocket and pulls out a mint imperial covered in fluff. 'Best be off,' she says.

A cloud of warblers flutter in and out of the naked pear tree behind our bedroom. Not a partridge in a pear tree, but one day Christmas will come and Bernard will be back. And he'll have even less idea of what to do with a howling baby than me. And I still have to hold in my pubic symphysis when I stand up, because my (now hairy) mount of Venus still pushes back in my hand. And I've got to get that cat gut out from my down-under, before it starts to infect.

I don't want to see our family doctor, he's a cold fish. (When I had bronchitis he gave me the same yellow antibiotics as Chérie the dog). People had difficult relations with their doctors in those days. No internet: the doctor was the fount of all wisdom, only he didn't tell you things, and in return, neither did the patient. Even Queen Victoria. She developed a fat stomach later in life after she'd popped out all those nine children and Albert was dead. At court they all thought it was gluttony - and she did have a remarkably quick shovelling action with her fork. (They noticed this because etiquette required that when the Queen had finished, then they too had to lay down their cutlery.) At the end of her life, she was really fat. In fact, Victoria had a massive growth in her stomach which stopped her wearing the girdles and corsets that had previously kept her trim. Her doctor knew nothing of this till he did an autopsy at her death and had a good poke around. Which begs the question, why did they do an autopsy on the old queen? Is this standard practice for monarchs or did they think that her eldest, Bertie, could stand it no longer and had finished her off, so desperate was he to be crowned Edward VII?

Like Victoria, I don't want my GP poking around down there, telling me not to make a fuss. So I change GPs, which causes a bit of a stir. Not the sort of thing you do in Ormskirk, everyone will know, but I go down Stanley Street (where else?) to see old Doctor Temple. 'May your daughters be like the polished corners of the Temple' it says somewhere in the psalms. I'm not quite sure what that means, but I find it strangely reassuring. Dr Temple has a proper look and what's more, incredibly, he tells me what he sees.

'Well,' he says, 'first they did an episiotomy, which is a cut, to make more room for the baby's head to come out, but then the cut tore all the way up your back passage. Forceps, no doubt. I'm not surprised you're sore,' he says. 'You've had a really big tear, a good, long way up the back passage.'

A big tear right up the back passage. No one mentioned that. No wonder it felt like passing a bolder down a constricted pipe.

Child birth: a rite of passage with no respect for your back passage, your middle passage or any other passage for that matter. No therapy offered.

So that was it. That was what had happened and no one thought to tell me.

Dr Temple takes a razor blade and carefully splices through the knots in the blackened cat gut, pulls them out with tweezers and drops them one by one into the kidney bowl.

'That should feel better,' he says straightening up, 'but it will take time.'

But I can now take little Benji round to my grandparents in the afternoon. I sit and watch Bonanza with my granny while my grandad rocks the crying baby wrapped in the white shawl she crocheted.

'The day Thou gavest Lord is ended

The darkness falls all o'er the land,' sings my grandad.

Back and forth he rocks him, patting his back and the baby stops crying and gazes up at him.

You can't ask for more. This is bliss.

All weddings are different, they say. All funerals are different. But what about a churching? Are they all different? It was definitely obligatory if we wanted to gather all the family together, later in the bleak midwinter, and christen the baby before we left for Marrakech.

'It is indeed advisable to get him christened before you leave for foreign parts,' says Reverend Roberts.

To be honest I can't remember much about it, only that I had to give thanks for being carried 'safely' (that's a matter of opinion) through the travails of childbirth. It was a short afternoon ceremony; mum was at school and my dad was at another 'meeting' in London, so I put on a very thick pad and pushed the pram slowly down the St Helens' Road, past Charlie's garage, past the Disraeli statue of Lord Beaconsfield, through the town and up the incline to Orme's kirk.

Ormskirk was changing, becoming quite cosmopolitan with the 'Acropolis Fish Bar' - fish and the very best chips in the region. But how did these Greeks end up in Ormskirk, selling Icelandic cod and chips to the English in 1976? What was their story? Did they flee the war in Cyprus? (When was the war in Cyprus?) I never thought to ask. There was also a new Chinese restaurant - migrants from Liverpool's Chinatown perhaps? The oldest in Europe. Or direct from China? Either way, they got themselves a bad reputation when Mrs Holmes, the biggest gossip at the Women's Institute, cut open the crunchy batter of a sweet and sour pork ball, to find only white bread inside. It was her fault really, not playing fair, because everyone knows the English just shovel their food into their mouths without paying attention to what they are eating.

The churching is an afternoon ceremony with only two old ladies in attendance. They whisper to each other as the baby's howls ricoché off the walls and the headless torso of Stanley, the earl of Derby turns in his tomb.

I hobble up the aisle.

'I'm fine,' I say to Reverend Roberts, waiting for me by the altar, 'I caught verrucas in Ormskirk General.'

It wasn't the only reason, though I couldn't tell him that, but it was true enough. For now that I can bend over I can see on the soles of my feet, red mounds surrounded by verruca spikes. But in the grand order of damage, verrucas are inconsequential.

Leaves fall,

seasons pass

but

memory

and

the moon

hold fast

In December, Bernard steps out of the Ormskirk mist, bronzed and athletic to bond with his two month old son (though we didn't know then that was what he was doing). And on their reunion, the baby pulls out all the stops. Lying on his changing mat, he peddles his little legs, blowing raspberries and gurgling all the while, so pleased was he to see his dad again. But Bernard has yet to discover the joys of broken nights, a wife with no libido and terry towelling nappies that leak all over your trousers. Mum said it would be a good idea to put a pair of plastic pants over the top of the nappies to contain any leakage, but there was no internet and we were all too exhausted to go to Mothercare in Liverpool. So Bernard was sent down to Ormskirk to see if he could find a pair of plastic pants in 'Boots the Chemist'.

'Do you have plastic knickers?' he asks the pretty young assistant, who flushes to the roots of her red hair and calls the manageress. Unfortunately, Bernard had never read Beryl Bainbridge.

Then we get to Christmas. There was a time when I never thought we would make it through to Christmas. And that's another incredible birthing story isn't it? This baby who was 'begotten not created'. No sex, no sperm and egg thing, no gametes splitting and dividing and growing - like an idea taking shape. But the word somehow became flesh.

My neighbour's 6-year-old daughter has a favourite book that she carries with her everywhere. *The Bible for Children*.

'Baby Jesus,' she says, 'it's the best story ever.'

After an immaculate conception (no sex), Mary his mother, was delivered of a son. He was not born out of her left ear, like Zeus when he gave birth to Athena.

This is surprisingly, when you think about it, given His

Madonna Litta, Leonardo Da Vinci hermitage Museum
St Petersburg. ©Commons.wiki.media.org

method of conception. Jesus was delivered by the normal route - no caesarian section, no divine intervention.

'How silently, how silently the wondrous gift is given.' The Christ child is born in silence, we are told. An easy birth apparently. No screaming or shouting or panting like a dog. Perhaps it was the three hours on a donkey to get to Nazareth that moved things along. But he was of woman born, he could empathise in a way that Athena never could. 'And he feeleth for our sadness, and he shareth in our gladness.' But the question remains, can the Virgin Mother still technically be considered a virgin once she had given birth by the vagina, the low road 'par la *voie basse'* as the French say? Obviously, the hymen must have been ruptured, mustn't it? The curtain torn, so no longer a virgin ... technically?

'Lo He abhors not the virgin's womb', the bible tells us, and clearly, he abhorred not the virgin's breast either. Although colostrum doesn't get a mention in the Christmas story, there are some twenty pictures of the Virgin Mary feeding her babe with her milk of human kindness. And I don't suppose the babe had any difficulty latching on to his mother's nipple. Most of these pictures show the Virgin with one bare breast and the babe looking archly round at the painter - otherwise if his head were buried in the breast, the viewer would see only the back of his head. In this one, by Leonardo da Vinci there is also a clever bit of fashion design by the artist, for Mary's bust.

But my favourite is by Jean Fouquet (1450) of the Virgin Mother and child, surrounded by angels, staring out, elegantly garbed, erect and respectable, except for one perfect breast, pert and alert, thrust towards us - no leaking or sagging, no submission to terrestrial gravity. Proud Mary. The mother stares at us, happy to display her perfectly rounded apple. After the eviction from the garden, Eve finally gets her revenge.

Madonna Lactans, by Jean Fouquet.
©Commons.wiki.media.org

The miracle is also how these artists imagined the Virgin and Child. How they conjured them up from their imagination and brought them to life. Like gametes separating and joining. An idea forming. Creation.

The very next day after Christmas, on the feast of Saint Stephen, comes the christening of our baby, in Orme's kirk.

Newly churched and standing beside my husband and the Earl of Stanley, (not the one who lost his head to Cromwell, the other one). Trying to come to terms with this state of motherhood and this heavy responsibility. Perhaps the presence of the turncoat Stanley, the first Earl of Derby, is a positive omen. He was a survivor. Treacherous, but a survivor. Perhaps everything will be alright with Stanley as ghostly godfather to this little scrap of humanity, yelling and twisting on this snowy Boxing Day, a brown stain spreading over his beautiful christening gown, despite the plastic knickers.

Bernard's cousins come from Paris and we take them out to the Wildfowl Trust at Martin Mere (an inland sea, named by the Normans in honour of Saint Martin, patron saint of blacksmiths, policemen and soldiers). We shiver in the cold and marvel at the black trumpeter swans that would break a man's arm if he approached their young.

Then it is time to leave, to set off as a family. The three of us. To Marrakech with no washing machine and all those nappies that will ferment in buckets, little brown bubbles rising to the surface. Back to cold nights in an unheated flat and to Radia, the cleaning lady who negotiates a pay rise when she sees the quantity of soiled terry towelling nappies she will have to wash. She hangs the washing out on the flat roof of the terrace above us, but one day she goes home without collecting it in and in the night, the whole lot gets pinched, which means we are short of nappies and babygrows and the French equivalent, *grenouillières* (little froggy outfits). Till mum comes out to visit in February with a collection of clothes from Mothercare. Dad comes too but he is acting strange, watching his waistline, refusing all the glorious Moroccan cakes and pastries. He even refuses the 'gazelle's horn of plenty', overflowing with the almond paste that he is so fond of. At every opportunity he strips off and attempts to sun bathe on our tiny balcony, somewhat constricted by the pink oleander bush in a pot. He says we should get rid of that bush. Oleander is poisonous and the baby might fall out of his buggy and eat it, he says ... and it would also give him more sunlight to bathe in.

He was behaving really strange, but we were too busy with the baby to notice. It was only later that the penny dropped. Benjamin, his first grandchild, was born in 1976 (I think you've got that by now). Two years later, Dad was gone. It wasn't as if he'd ever got up at night to hush the screaming child. But it didn't take him long to clear off, running after his lost youth. There was a farewell photo of him in the *Ormskirk Advertiser,* sitting on his desk, shirt collar open, showing off his suntanned bald head (that twenty years later would be covered with BCCs - that had to be hunted down and burnt by the NHS).

Dad ditched Mum and us and Edge Hill College and Ormskirk. He was off to the smoke ...and his new found mistress who was in search of a husband since she'd got a divorce. An innocent abroad my old Dad, and she soon worked out how to press his buttons and undo his flies.

We brought the Maclaren buggy back with us to Marrakech but I couldn't go out with the baby without collecting a retinue of young lads, tugging at my sleeve, wanting to sell me something. We waited in the flat till Bernard came home from school before going out for a walk amongst the purple bougainvillea in the early evening sun. Or we would go and watch him playing tennis on the 'clay' courts (in reality, red bricks ground down to fine powder) where he would disappear in a cloud of red dust.

Morocco is a hot country during the day. It has stone floors and no heating. But at night in the winter, it is bitterly cold when you get out of bed to feed and change a baby. Yet it is somehow comforting to know that the rest of Marrakech is also awake as the *muezzin* calls the faithful to prayer over the loud speakers on the top of the minaret. There are other creatures that do not sleep either: fat brown cockroaches venture out from behind the skirting boards, to scuttle over the floor and the bedside tables. They are shy creatures which I rarely see in the daylight, except for that one time when I was sitting on the bidet, facing the taps, legs straddled, swilling warm water over my still tender nether parts, when two long feelers twitched out of the overflow hole, the cockroach's globular eyeballs rolling at the sight of my naked down-there. My screams echo off the walls as I arise from the bidet - another Birth of Venus, emerging from the waterhole and trying not to slip on the cold tiled floor.

CHAPTER 12

It's the Randomness, Isn't It?

*B*ut nowadays it's better, isn't it? It's got to be better. When you have a baby, you hand over control of your body, your baby, both your lives. The belief in the NHS used to be the nearest thing to a national religion. Let's hope that you find yourself with people you know and trust, like the wonderful Yorkshire midwives, we see nowadays on TV. Those compassionate, young women on call day and night, rushing to your home, whenever you need them, ready to fulfil your birth plan and trying so hard to give you the amazing experience that you have imagined and that will stay with you for the rest of your life.

Or, you might not be so lucky. It's the randomness of it, isn't it? The what if? What if you don't get a caring Yorkshire midwife, but end up in an old workhouse hospital? What if you end up in an institution with a bullying, toxic culture, that blames the mothers when things go wrong.

Senior midwife and community activist, Donna Ockenden, led the biggest review of maternity services in the history of the NHS (2000 - 2019), into the Shrewsbury and Telford Trust. Initially her committee thought they had 23 cases to investigate, but there turned out to be nearer 2,000. And the report they published in March 2022 beggars belief. It documents the horrendous failures and toxic culture of this trust. Nine mothers died in childbirth, along with more than

200 babies who lost their young lives.

The ideology was to keep caesarian sections as low as possible, preferring "normal births", by the low road, (la voie basse), a vaginal birth, whatever the pregnancy. Caesarean sections were delayed too long, babies were starved of oxygen and were born with brain damage. The committee found a culture of silence and non-cooperation, with doctors, nurses and midwives being told there would be consequences for their jobs if they cooperated with the enquiry.

Worse still was the culture of undermining and bullying the mothers, blaming them when things went wrong: "You probably smoked, so it's your fault."

The Shrewsbury and Telford Trust and the NHS refused to investigate and learn from their mistakes, even though in 2015 there had been a similar enquiry at Morecambe Bay, just down the road from Ormskirk, which concluded that this same culture of "natural births" had contributed to "poor outcomes" - that's a great euphemism, isn't it? A brain damaged child and a dead mother is only a 'poor outcome'. Well, that's not so bad then, is it?

This shocking culture in Telford and Shrewsbury only came to light finally because the families complained and kept on complaining, till they got Jeremy Hunt, then Health secretary, to commission this full independent investigation. At the enquiry many of the families said they thought they were the only ones who had suffered in this way, at the hands of our national health service...

The NHS now says it is sorry and has apologised for these 'poor outcomes'. Nevertheless, it is estimated that there are 1,000 preventable infant deaths every year in Britain.

Hungary and Slovenia have lower infant mortality rates than Britain.

There is no shortage of heartache in this world - but spare a thought for these poor mothers, losing their babies, or having their babies damaged by the very institution that is meant to protect them ... and then being told it was their fault, and having to live with this damage for the rest of their lives.

It has taken me 46 years to tell my birthing story with the NHS. There must be many more similar stories waiting to be told..

June 2016

Queuing at border control behind an elderly couple off the flight from Alicante: The woman turns around, 'You got any of them sick bags left darlin'? She asks. 'My John here's feeling a bit queasy... too much brandy, not enough coke.'

I open my rucksack and fumble.

'Write on all of 'em, did ya?' she asks. 'Shopping lists?' The woman leans in, pulls a moon bag out of my sack and hands it to her John who wretches noisily into one of my chapters.

'Better out than in,' she says, handing him a tissue. 'I used to do that, shopping lists, when we come over from Benidorm ... Baked beans, Marmite, Cadbury's Milk Tray, Paxo stuffing ... Golden Syrup and Oxo Cubes. But now they got everything out there. Benidorm. Real home from home.'

'Right,' I say wondering if there is any way I can salvage my chapter.

'Lovely out there. Sun. Food.'

'Cheap booze,' mumbles John.

'Good for me bones,' she says.

'Just back to Britain for the summer?' I ask.

'Oh no. We wouldn't miss the summer in Spain. Not for nothing. You can rely on Spain. It's gorgeous.'

'Er viva Espana!' sings John perking up. 'We're just back for the referendum.'

'We want our sovereignty back,' says his wife.

'Vote leave,' says John.

'That's what you should do duck,' says the woman. 'Vote leave. All them foreigners. Nicking 350 million every week from our National Health Service. The envy of the world that is.'

Printed in Great Britain
by Amazon

22081945R10086